ANNE WILLAN'S
LOOK&COOK

Delicious Desserts

ANNE WILLAN'S
LOOK & COOK
Delicious Desserts

DORLING KINDERSLEY
LONDON • NEW YORK • STUTTGART

A DORLING KINDERSLEY BOOK

Created and Produced by
CARROLL & BROWN LIMITED
5 Lonsdale Road
London NW6 6RA

Editorial Director Jeni Wright
Contributing Editor Norma MacMillan
Editors Julia Alcock
Jane Middleton

Managing Art Editor Lyndel Donaldson
Art Editor Mary Staples
Designer Alan Watt
Production Editor Wendy Rogers

First American Edition, 1993
10 9 8 7 6 5 4 3 2 1

Published in the United States by
Dorling Kindersley, Inc., 232 Madison Avenue
New York, New York 10016

Willan, Anne.
   Delicious desserts. – 1st American ed.
      p.   cm. – (Anne Willan's Look and cook)
   Includes index.
   ISBN 1-56458-300-7
   1. Desserts I. Title. II. Series: Willan, Anne. Look & cook.
TX773.W66   1993
641.8'6 – dc20   93-3087
                                                       CIP

Reproduced by Colourscan, Singapore
Printed and bound in Italy by A. Mondadori, Verona

CONTENTS

DELICIOUS DESSERTS

THE LOOK & COOK APPROACH

Welcome to **Delicious Desserts** and the *Look & Cook* series. These volumes are designed to be the simplest, most informative cookbooks you'll ever own. They are the closest I can come to sharing my personal techniques for cooking my favorite recipes without actually being with you in the kitchen.

EQUIPMENT

Equipment and ingredients often determine whether you can cook a particular dish, so *Look & Cook* illustrates everything you need at the beginning of each recipe. You'll see at a glance how long a recipe takes to cook and how many servings it makes, what the finished dish looks like, and how much preparation can be done ahead. When you start to cook, you'll find the preparation and cooking are organized into easy-to-follow steps. Each stage has its own color coding, and everything is shown in photographs with brief text accompanying each step. You will never be in doubt as to what it is you are doing, why you are doing it, or how it should look.

INGREDIENTS

🍽 SERVES 4–6   🥣 WORK TIME 25–35 MINUTES   🍲 COOKING TIME 20–30 MINUTES

I've also included helpful hints and ideas under "Anne Says." These may suggest an alternative ingredient or piece of equipment, explain the reason for using a certain method, or offer advice on mastering a particular technique. Similarly, if there is a crucial stage in a recipe when things can go wrong, I've included some warnings called "Take Care."

Many of the photographs are annotated to pinpoint why a certain piece of equipment works best, or how food should look at that stage of cooking. Because presentation is so important, there is a picture of the finished dish at the end of each recipe, often with serving suggestions.

Thanks to all this information, you can't go wrong. I'll be with you every step of the way. So please come with me into the kitchen to look, cook, and enjoy some **Delicious Desserts**.

WHY DESSERTS?

Luscious fruits, tawny caramel, crisp pastries, smooth chocolate, meltingly rich creams – we all have our favorite flavor and texture for dessert. And some of us will admit that appetizers and main dishes are simply overtures to the most important course of any meal – dessert! A delicious dessert forms the grand finale of the finest dinner.

RECIPE CHOICE

In this volume you will find a collection of delectable desserts to suit any menu. Make your choice according to the occasion, the number of guests, and the season. When the weather is hot, a gem-toned fruit terrine or a refreshing fruit sorbet makes a great ending to a meal. On a cool autumn night, finish dinner with crisp Apple and Almond Galettes, or a feather-light Grand Marnier Soufflé. Cheesecake or Baklava are casual do-ahead desserts to please a hungry group at an informal buffet, while an elegant dinner will reach a dramatic conclusion with Crêpes Suzette.

COLD DESSERTS

Cold desserts, whether they are served chilled or at room temperature, are ideal for entertaining, as most of them may be made ahead. *Tiramisù*: this Italian treat of coffee- and liqueur-soaked sponge cake fingers cloaked in a creamy mascarpone cheese mixture is always a popular choice. *Rum and Chocolate Tiramisù*: rum-soaked sponge cake fingers and mascarpone are layered in individual dishes, then topped with grated chocolate. *Mosaic Fruit Terrine*: colorful chunks of fresh fruit are bound with a sweet white wine gelatin, to be sliced and served with an orange-mint sauce. *Tri-Color Terrine*: a delicate pear purée surrounds orange, green, and red fruit. *Baklava*: delicate phyllo pastry is layered with spiced walnuts and pistachios, then moistened with a honey syrup. *Phyllo Nut Rolls*: crisp individual rolled phyllo pastries hold a filling of chopped nuts and spices. *Orange and Cinnamon Crème Brûlée*: toasted cinnamon and fresh orange flavor a smooth baked custard, topped with crisp caramel. *Lemon Crème Brûlée with Blackberries*: a layer of tart blackberries lies beneath lemon-flavored custard and

caramel. *Chocolate Decadence with Raspberry Coulis*: a rich, moist cake designed for true chocolate lovers. A contrasting raspberry coulis and a dollop of whipped cream are the only adornments. *Chocolate Decadence with Passion Fruit Sauce*: an unusual pairing of chocolate and passion fruit makes a delightful change. *Ginger Cheesecake*: spicy stem ginger enlivens this classic, creamy cheesecake. *Sour Cream and Fruit Cheesecake*: a layer of sour cream and fresh fruit tops a lemon-scented cheesecake filling. *Spanish Rolled Sponge Cake*: a moist lemon sponge cake is rolled around rum-spiked chocolate ganache, then sliced to show a pinwheel pattern. *Individual Sponge Cake Rolls*: these miniature Spanish rolls are a tempting size and shape. *Hazelnut Meringue Gâteau (Dacquoise)*: perfect for special occasions, this elegant cake features layers of hazelnut meringue and kirsch-flavored butter cream.

Almond Meringue Gâteau: toasted almonds and Armagnac give a wonderful flavor to this layered dessert. *Exotic Fruit in Tulip Cookie Cups*: crisp, delicate cookie containers hold a mixture of exotic fruits, perfumed with rosewater. *Wafer Towers with Exotic Fruit*: wafers are sandwiched with fruit and cream into appealing "towers." *Rum-Soaked Ring Cake (Savarin)*: a rich yeast dough ring cake is soaked in rum syrup and served with seasonal fresh red fruit and Chantilly cream. *Rum Babas*: dried currants are added to yeast dough, which is baked in individual molds. *Chestnut Napoleons*: light pastry cream and crumbled candied chestnuts are layered between buttery bands of crisp puff pastry. *Chocolate Napoleons*: dark chocolate flavors the pastry cream filling of these Napoleons. *Coconut and Pineapple Mousse Cake*: a creamy mousse made with fresh pineapple is layered with tender coconut sponge cake. *Citrus Mousse Cake*: tangy lemon and orange star in this refreshing gâteau.

FROZEN DESSERTS

Frozen desserts are a real boon for entertaining, since they are invariably made well in advance. Many frozen desserts provide a perfect base for attractive decoration, and all the concoctions in this book make colorful presentations. *Trio of Sorbets*: ripe, fresh fruits – raspberry, pear, and peach – are puréed, then combined with sugar syrup, to transform them into refreshing sorbets. *Panaché of Sorbets*: tangerine, apple, and strawberry are tempting flavors too. *Amaretti and Chocolate Bombe*: rich Amaretto ice cream encloses a frozen center of Amaretti cookies and chocolate. Warm chocolate sauce completes this luxurious combination. *Spiced Honey and Cherry Bombe*: red cherries are concealed in the center of honey ice cream, served with a cherry sauce. *Iced Peach Soufflé*: a fresh peach mousse is frozen in a soufflé dish, then decorated with peach slices and confectioners' sugar. *Iced Peach Parfait with Blueberries*: peach mousse is swirled with a blueberry compote, frozen, and served in scoops with poached peach slices. *Strawberry Ice Cream in a Flower Ice Bowl*: fresh strawberry ice cream is served in a bowl made from flowers and leaves embedded in ice. *Strawberry-Rose Petal Bowl*: rose petals and leaves are used to make an ice bowl, which is then filled with fresh strawberries and strawberry ice cream.

HOT DESSERTS

Warm or hot desserts may range from a simple melted chocolate fondue to the culinary drama of French crêpes flamed with Grand Marnier.
Chocolate Nut Fondue: fresh fruit and shortbread cookies are dipped in warm, satiny cinnamon-flavored chocolate, then in chopped pecans. *Chocolate Coconut Fondue*: orange flavors the chocolate in this fondue. The coated fruits are then dipped into toasted coconut, giving a tropical accent. *Baked Alaska*: warm, toasted meringue provides a surprising contrast to a frozen interior of vanilla ice cream, strawberries, and moist *génoise* sponge cake. *Individual Coffee Baked Alaskas*: individual meringue-topped Baked Alaskas are filled with coffee ice cream. *Crêpes Suzette*: French techniques are put to spectacular effect in this classic dessert. *Chocolate and Orange Crêpes*: cocoa-flavored crêpes are sautéed with orange butter, flamed, and sprinkled with grated chocolate. *Apple Soufflé Crêpes*: an apple soufflé mixture is encased in individual crêpes, then baked until puffed and golden. *Apple and Almond Galettes*: flaky puff pastry rounds are covered with almond paste and thinly sliced apples, then baked until caramelized. *Rhubarb Galettes*: sticks of rhubarb are arranged like the spokes of a wheel on top of puff pastry rounds. *Grand Marnier Soufflé*: this light and airy soufflé, laced with orange liqueur, and served with an orange compote, is ideal for an elegant dinner. *Hot Coffee Soufflé*: coffee soufflé is served with cardamom-spiced cream.

EQUIPMENT

None of the desserts in this book requires highly specialized or costly equipment. However, many of the recipes call for a particular size or shape of pan or mold, and this is crucial to the success of the finished dish. Do not be tempted to change them: using the appropriate cake pan ensures even cooking and browning in the oven, while a mold of the correct dimensions and volume produces bombes, soufflés, and terrines with the right shape and texture.

A springform cake pan, with its straight side and removable base, makes the graham cracker crust in Ginger Cheesecake easy to shape and is useful for constructing the even layers of Coconut Pineapple Mousse Cake. Baking sheets, used in a range of recipes from Spanish Rolled Sponge Cake to Hazelnut Meringue Gâteau, should be as heavy as possible so they conduct the heat evenly and do not warp. You'll need ovenproof dishes in various sizes, from small ramekins for individual crèmes brûlées to the larger, deep soufflé dishes essential for both hot and cold soufflés.

Whipped, whisked, and beaten mixtures are important components of many desserts in this book. A sturdy electric mixer takes the effort out of many recipes. A hand-held electric mixer is useful for making light batters and for whipping cream. Egg whites reach maximum volume when they are whipped by hand in a stainless-steel bowl with a balloon whisk, but you can also use an electric mixer, preferably with a metal bowl.

You will need an ice-cream maker for sorbets, ice creams, and other frozen desserts. Machines range from sophisticated versions that chill as well as churn the mixture to hand-cranked models. A food processor makes quick work of puréeing fruit and it is also useful for chopping nuts and chocolate. For general chopping and cutting tasks, a small paring knife and a larger chef's knife are indispensable; they should be sharpened regularly, and always stored with care. A long serrated knife is ideal for slicing fragile cakes and pastries, like Chestnut Napoleons or the sponge fingers in Tiramisù.

Saucepans of various sizes are used for making pastry creams, custards, and chocolate ganache; make sure your pans have a heavy base so that delicate mixtures cook evenly without scorching. I like to make crêpes in a traditional, shallow, cast-iron frying pan, but a small non-stick frying pan gives good results too.

Small items play a large role in dessert-making. A good vegetable peeler is invaluable for peeling fruit and for paring the zest from lemons and oranges. A pastry brush makes buttering pans and molds easy and is useful for brushing excess flour from pastry, provided the brush is completely dry. The presentation of desserts is improved immeasurably when you use a pastry bag and tube, often in a star shape, for shaping meringue and whipped cream. When cooking sugar syrup to the soft ball or hard ball stage, a candy thermometer is helpful, though not essential.

INGREDIENTS

Sugar and flour are the basic ingredients for most desserts, together with dairy products such as eggs, milk, cream, and butter. These building blocks provide the foundation for the "starring" ingredients – fresh fruits, which are puréed, poached, or used raw; deep, rich chocolate, which may be melted, grated, or mixed with cream; and nuts, particularly walnuts and pecans, which provide an appealing crunch as well as flavor in desserts such as Baklava and Chocolate Nut Fondue.

Wine, liqueurs, and spirits add a punchy note to many desserts. A honey-sweet dessert wine, such as Sauternes, marries well with fresh fruit in Mosaic Fruit Terrine. Rum-spiked syrup soaks a buttery yeast ring cake and its diminutive cousins, Rum Babas. Grand Marnier is featured in a hot soufflé and flamed in the French classic, Crêpes Suzette, while Tiramisù benefits from a generous splash of coffee-flavored Tia Maria or Kahlúa.

More unusual ingredients featured in this book include the French specialty *marrons glacés* (candied chestnuts), and peppery-sweet stem ginger. Even the petals and leaves of edible flowers make their appearance in a flower ice bowl.

TECHNIQUES

The right techniques are more important for successful desserts than for any other branch of cooking. None of them is difficult, but they must be done correctly. You will find them "demystified" by the step-by-step pictures in this book, and you will learn to prepare many of the basics of pastry and desserts, such as egg custard, pastry cream, poached fruit, and gelatin. More advanced techniques, such as whipping up a sponge cake, using phyllo pastry, making puff pastry, and making ice cream and sorbet, are described in easy-to-follow stages. With this approach, potentially intimidating recipes – Baked Alaska or a hot soufflé – are achievable even for beginners! Many important techniques used in these recipes are illustrated in detail in special "How-To" boxes throughout the book. These include making Chantilly cream; filling a pastry bag; piping cream decorations; lining a cake pan; peeling, pitting, and cubing mangoes; peeling and sectioning citrus fruit; toasting and skinning nuts; softening and melting gelatin; making candied lemon zest; separating eggs; whisking egg whites; and folding mixtures together.

TIRAMISU

🍴 SERVES 8–10   🥄 WORK TIME 35–40 MINUTES*   ☕ BAKING TIME 30–40 MINUTES

EQUIPMENT

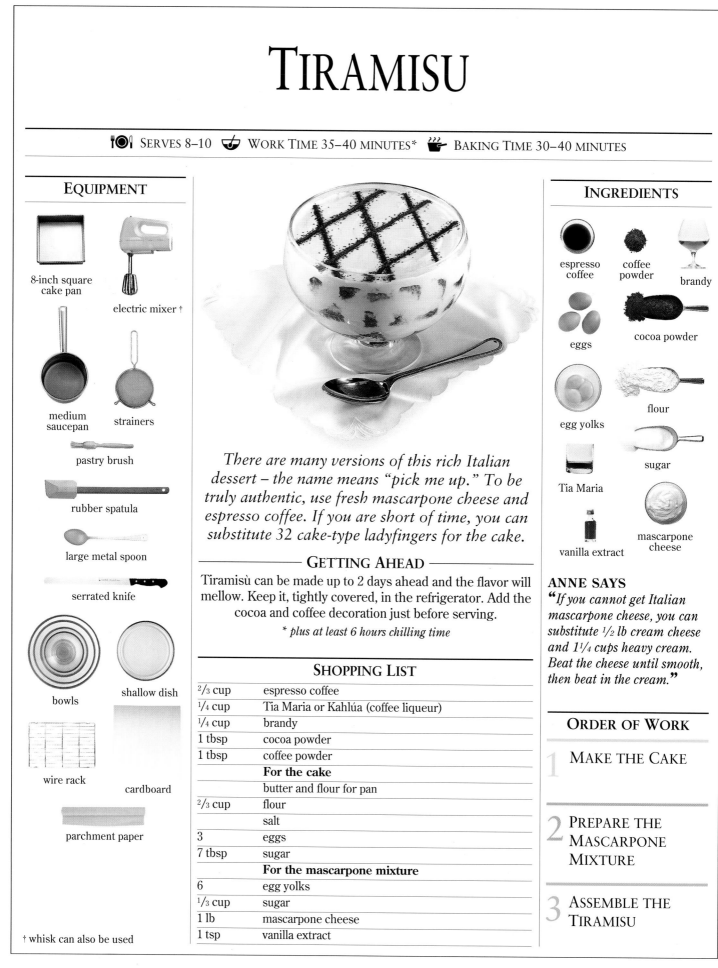

- 8-inch square cake pan
- electric mixer †
- medium saucepan
- strainers
- pastry brush
- rubber spatula
- large metal spoon
- serrated knife
- bowls
- shallow dish
- wire rack
- cardboard
- parchment paper

† whisk can also be used

INGREDIENTS

- espresso coffee
- coffee powder
- brandy
- eggs
- cocoa powder
- egg yolks
- flour
- Tia Maria
- sugar
- vanilla extract
- mascarpone cheese

There are many versions of this rich Italian dessert – the name means "pick me up." To be truly authentic, use fresh mascarpone cheese and espresso coffee. If you are short of time, you can substitute 32 cake-type ladyfingers for the cake.

GETTING AHEAD

Tiramisù can be made up to 2 days ahead and the flavor will mellow. Keep it, tightly covered, in the refrigerator. Add the cocoa and coffee decoration just before serving.

* plus at least 6 hours chilling time

SHOPPING LIST

²/₃ cup	espresso coffee
¼ cup	Tia Maria or Kahlúa (coffee liqueur)
¼ cup	brandy
1 tbsp	cocoa powder
1 tbsp	coffee powder
	For the cake
	butter and flour for pan
²/₃ cup	flour
	salt
3	eggs
7 tbsp	sugar
	For the mascarpone mixture
6	egg yolks
¹/₃ cup	sugar
1 lb	mascarpone cheese
1 tsp	vanilla extract

ANNE SAYS

"If you cannot get Italian mascarpone cheese, you can substitute ½ lb cream cheese and 1¼ cups heavy cream. Beat the cheese until smooth, then beat in the cream."

ORDER OF WORK

1 MAKE THE CAKE

2 PREPARE THE MASCARPONE MIXTURE

3 ASSEMBLE THE TIRAMISU

1 MAKE THE CAKE

1 Heat the oven to 350°F. Butter the cake pan and line the bottom with parchment paper. Butter the paper. Sprinkle in 2 tbsp flour and turn the pan to coat the inside; tap the pan upside down to remove excess flour.

Use pastry brush to apply thin, even layer of butter

2 Sift the flour with a pinch of salt; set aside. Put the eggs in a large bowl and beat with the electric mixer for a few seconds to mix. Add the sugar. Continue beating at high speed until the mixture is pale and thick and leaves a ribbon trail when the beaters are lifted, about 5 minutes.

ANNE SAYS
"*If using a whisk, set the bowl over a pan of hot, but not boiling, water and whisk vigorously, about 10 minutes.*"

Use rubber spatula to scoop batter from bowl

3 Sift about one-third of the flour over the egg mixture and fold them together: cut down into the center of the bowl with the rubber spatula, scoop under the egg mixture, and turn it over in a rolling motion. At the same time, with the other hand, turn the bowl counter-clockwise. Fold in the remaining flour in 2 batches.

4 Pour the batter into the prepared cake pan. Tap the pan on a work surface to level the batter and knock out any air bubbles.

5 Bake in the heated oven until the cake has risen and is just firm to the touch, 30–40 minutes. Unmold the cake onto the wire rack. Peel off the lining paper and let the cake cool.

2 PREPARE THE MASCARPONE MIXTURE

1 Put the egg yolks and sugar in a large heatproof bowl and beat them to mix, using the electric mixer or a hand whisk.

2 Set the bowl over a saucepan of hot, but not simmering, water. Whisk the mixture until pale and thick enough to leave a ribbon trail, 3–5 minutes.

3 Take the bowl from the pan of hot water and continue beating until the mixture has cooled slightly, 1–2 minutes. Let cool completely.

4 Combine the mascarpone and vanilla extract in another bowl and stir with the rubber spatula until smooth and creamy.

For maximum effect when folding, scoop thoroughly under both mixtures

5 Add the egg yolk and sugar mixture to the mascarpone, and fold them together with the rubber spatula until evenly blended.

3 ASSEMBLE THE TIRAMISU

1 With the serrated knife, cut the cake crosswise in half. Slice each half horizontally into 2 equal layers, leaving them in place. Cut the cake layers crosswise into 32 fingers about 1 inch wide.

Moistened cake fingers are placed close together to form bottom layer of dessert

2 Combine the espresso coffee, Tia Maria, and brandy in the shallow dish. Dip each of the cake fingers, cut-side down, in the coffee mixture to absorb some of the liquid, then place in the bottom of a large serving dish. Continue to moisten one-third of the cake fingers to make a single layer. Sprinkle them with 2 tbsp of the remaining coffee mixture.

3 Spoon one-third of the mascarpone mixture over the cake fingers to cover them completely.

4 Continue layering the moistened cake fingers and mascarpone mixture, ending with a layer of mascarpone mixture. Smooth the surface with the large metal spoon. Cover and chill at least 6 hours.

5 Mix together the cocoa and coffee powders. Cut 4 strips of cardboard and lay them across the tiramisù dish at even intervals. Sift the coffee mixture over the top to form lines. Lift off the strips; repeat at right angles to make a criss-cross pattern.

ANNE SAYS
"If you cannot get powdered coffee, finely crush instant coffee granules between 2 spoons."

🍴 **TO SERVE**
Serve the tiramisù directly from the dish, scooping out each portion with a large serving spoon.

Coffee and cocoa powders decorate tiramisù

VARIATION
RUM AND CHOCOLATE TIRAMISU
Rum-flavored individual tiramisù are topped with grated chocolate.

1 Substitute 33–36 packaged cake-type ladyfingers, total weight about 7 oz, for the cake fingers.
2 Make the mascarpone mixture as directed in the main recipe.
3 Make the coffee mixture as directed, using rum instead of the Tia Maria.
4 Moisten the ladyfingers in the coffee mixture and layer with the mascarpone mixture as directed, using individual dessert bowls. Cover the bowls and chill, at least 6 hours.
5 Just before serving, hold a 2 oz piece of semisweet chocolate in a piece of parchment paper or foil and work it against the coarsest grid of a grater, letting the grated chocolate fall onto a sheet of parchment paper or a plate.
6 Sprinkle the top of each tiramisù with grated chocolate and serve immediately.

Rich mascarpone cheese mixture is layered with cake fingers

MOSAIC FRUIT TERRINE

🍽️ SERVES 6 🥣 WORK TIME 30–40 MINUTES ❄️ CHILLING TIME AT LEAST 6½ HOURS

EQUIPMENT

5-cup enameled terrine mold †

chef's knife

small knife

bowls

wide metal spatula

citrus juicer

small strainer

ladle

whisk

wooden spoon

serrated knife

saucepans

chopping board

† porcelain or glass terrine mold can also be used

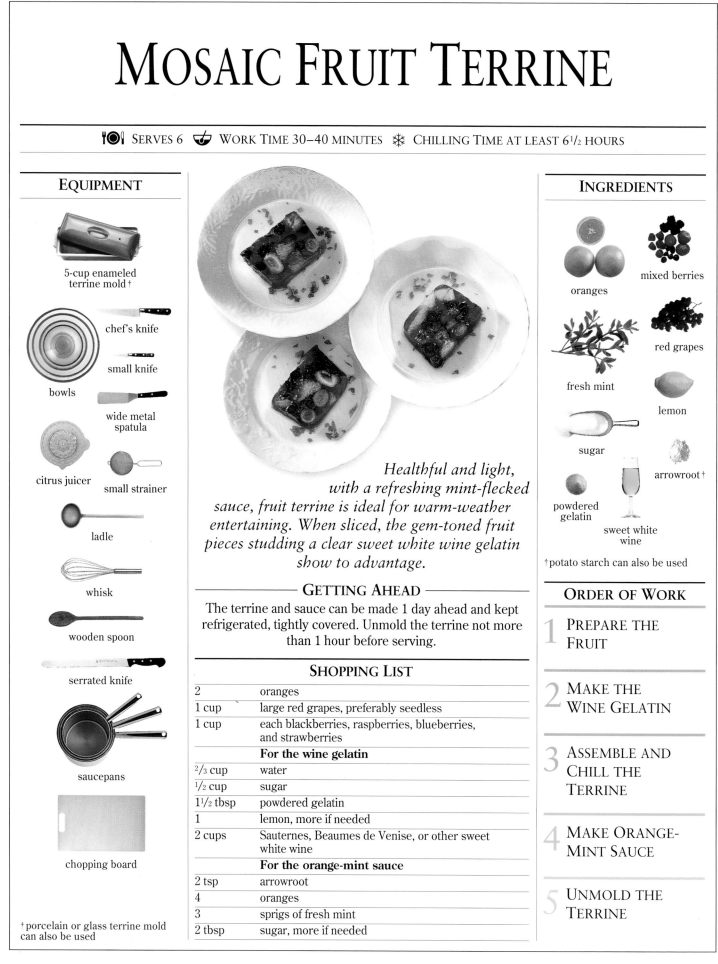

Healthful and light, with a refreshing mint-flecked sauce, fruit terrine is ideal for warm-weather entertaining. When sliced, the gem-toned fruit pieces studding a clear sweet white wine gelatin show to advantage.

GETTING AHEAD

The terrine and sauce can be made 1 day ahead and kept refrigerated, tightly covered. Unmold the terrine not more than 1 hour before serving.

SHOPPING LIST

2	oranges
1 cup	large red grapes, preferably seedless
1 cup	each blackberries, raspberries, blueberries, and strawberries
	For the wine gelatin
²/₃ cup	water
½ cup	sugar
1½ tbsp	powdered gelatin
1	lemon, more if needed
2 cups	Sauternes, Beaumes de Venise, or other sweet white wine
	For the orange-mint sauce
2 tsp	arrowroot
4	oranges
3	sprigs of fresh mint
2 tbsp	sugar, more if needed

INGREDIENTS

oranges

mixed berries

red grapes

fresh mint

lemon

sugar

arrowroot †

powdered gelatin

sweet white wine

† potato starch can also be used

ORDER OF WORK

1 PREPARE THE FRUIT

2 MAKE THE WINE GELATIN

3 ASSEMBLE AND CHILL THE TERRINE

4 MAKE ORANGE-MINT SAUCE

5 UNMOLD THE TERRINE

14

1 PREPARE THE FRUIT

1 With the small knife, slice off top and bottom of each orange. Cut away skin and white pith, following the curve of the fruit.

Remove all bitter pith from orange

Set fruit upright and hold steady with fingertips

2 Holding the orange over a bowl to catch the juice, slide the knife down one side of a section to cut it free of the membrane. Cut down the other side and scoop out the section. Repeat with the remaining sections, turning back the membrane like the pages of a book. Squeeze the leftover orange membrane over the bowl to catch the remaining juice.

3 Pull the grapes from the stems. Pick over the berries, washing them only if they are dirty. Hull strawberries; if they are large, cut them in half.

Fruit should be firm so it will not weep juice into gelatin

If washing berries, do not soak them or they will become soggy

HOW TO SOFTEN AND MELT POWDERED GELATIN

Gelatin must be used carefully because it easily cooks into strings, or forms lumps when added to other mixtures.

1 To soften gelatin: pour water or other specified liquid into a small saucepan and sprinkle the gelatin evenly on top.

2 Let soak about 5 minutes; the gelatin will soften to a spongy consistency.

3 To melt the gelatin: warm the saucepan over very low heat, or set it in a large bowl of hot water. Heat gently without stirring, shaking the pan occasionally, until pourable, 1–2 minutes. Use warm melted gelatin as directed in individual recipes.

! TAKE CARE !
Do not stir the gelatin during melting or it may form strings.

2 MAKE THE WINE GELATIN

1 Put 6 tbsp of the water in a small saucepan, add the sugar, and heat until dissolved, stirring occasionally. Bring to a boil and simmer 5 minutes. Meanwhile, soften the gelatin in the remaining water in another small pan, then melt it (see box, left).

2 Add the melted gelatin while still warm to the sugar syrup and stir until thoroughly mixed.

Sweet wine adds rich color

3 Squeeze the juice from the lemon. Stir half of the lemon juice and all the wine into the gelatin mixture. Taste, adding more lemon juice if needed. Reserve the remaining juice.

3 ASSEMBLE AND CHILL THE TERRINE

1 Using the ladle, pour enough of the wine gelatin into the mold to make a ½-inch layer. Refrigerate until set, about 30 minutes. Reserve the remaining wine gelatin at room temperature.

First layer of wine gelatin is set without fruit

2 Strain the juice from the orange sections and reserve. With your hands, gently toss the orange sections, grapes, and berries together in a bowl.

3 Add the fruit to the terrine in a random pattern, pressing it down gently with the back of your hand.

Mix with hand so fruit is not crushed

4 Slowly ladle the remaining wine gelatin into the mold. Gently shake and tap the mold so that the wine gelatin fills in all the spaces between the fruit. Cover and refrigerate until set, at least 6 hours.

Add wine gelatin gradually so all air pockets are filled

4 MAKE ORANGE-MINT SAUCE

1 In a small bowl, combine the arrowroot with the strained juice from sectioning the oranges. Blend together to form a smooth paste.

2 Squeeze the juice from the 4 oranges; there should be about 1½ cups. Strain the orange juice into a small saucepan.

3 Add 2 mint sprigs, the reserved lemon juice, and the sugar to the orange juice in the saucepan.

4 Bring the juice mixture just to a boil. Simmer about 1 minute, then remove and discard the mint sprigs.

Sauce thickens as soon as arrowroot mixture is added

Arrowroot forms smooth paste when mixed with cold liquid

5 Whisk the arrowroot paste into the simmering orange juice mixture to thicken it. Remove the saucepan from the heat and let the sauce cool.

6 Meanwhile, strip the leaves from the remaining mint sprig and pile them on the chopping board. With the chef's knife, coarsely chop the leaves. Stir the chopped mint into the sauce. Taste the sauce, and add more sugar or lemon juice if you like.

5 UNMOLD THE TERRINE

1 Dip the mold into a bowl of warm water 5–10 seconds, then dry the base. With your fingers, gently ease the fruit terrine away from the edges of the mold.

ANNE SAYS
"*Gently pull the terrine from the edges of the mold to break airlock.*"

Terrine should loosen easily after dipping mold in warm water

2 Set a chopping board on top of the mold and, holding the mold and board firmly together, turn them over so the terrine falls out onto the board.

🍴 TO SERVE

Cut the terrine across into slices, using the serrated knife with a gentle sawing motion. With the help of the wide metal spatula, transfer the slices to dessert plates. Spoon a little of the orange-mint sauce around the slices.

Seasonal fruits, in contrasting colors, make an appealing presentation

VARIATION
TRI-COLOR TERRINE

Here, pears are poached until tender, then puréed to hold the orange, green, and red fruit together.

1 Omit the blackberries, blueberries, and red grapes. Combine 2 cups water, ¹/₂ cup sugar, and the zest of 1 lemon in a saucepan. Heat until the sugar has dissolved; bring to a boil.
2 Peel 4 pears (total weight about 1¹/₂ lb) with a vegetable peeler, rubbing each one with a cut lemon so it does not discolor, then cut out the flower and stem ends with a small knife. Cut the pears lengthwise in half, and scoop out the cores with a melon baller or a small teaspoon.
3 Add the pear halves to the sugar syrup, cut-sides up. Press a round of parchment paper and a heatproof plate on top so the pears are completely submerged in the syrup.

4 Cover the pan and simmer gently until the pears are very tender, 25–35 minutes, depending on ripeness.
5 Let the pears cool in the poaching syrup, then remove them with a slotted spoon and purée in a food processor or blender. Stir in enough of the poaching syrup to make 3 cups purée. Work the pear purée through a strainer to remove all the fibers.
6 Prepare 2 large oranges as directed. Use 3 cups raspberries and strawberries only, and prepare as directed. Use seedless green grapes instead of red grapes, and cut them in half. Gently toss the fruit together.
7 Make the gelatin mixture as directed, replacing the wine and sugar syrup with the pear purée.
8 Set the first layer of gelatin as directed. Add the prepared fruit and the remaining gelatin to the terrine in alternating layers so that the gelatin flows evenly throughout. Chill the terrine as directed. Meanwhile, make the orange-mint sauce as directed.
9 Unmold the terrine, and cut into slices. Serve with the sauce, and decorate each plate with a mint sprig, if you like.

Orange-mint sauce picks up flavor of fruit terrine

BAKLAVA

EQUIPMENT

small knife

pastry brush

9- x 13-inch baking pan

chef's knife

bowls

2 dish towels

wooden spoon

citrus juicer

metal spatula

saucepans

candy thermometer

metal skewer

chopping board

INGREDIENTS

phyllo dough

walnut pieces

ground cinnamon

unsalted butter

honey

lemon

shelled pistachio nuts

ground cloves

sugar

orange-flower water †

† vanilla extract can also be used

This crispy Middle Eastern confection, filled with chopped nuts and spices and drenched with honey syrup, has long been a favorite with our family. Phyllo dough is readily available in ethnic groceries and in some supermarkets. It is easy to use provided you keep it moist while assembling the pastries.

GETTING AHEAD

The pastries can be made up to 5 days before serving. Store in an airtight container; the flavor will mellow.

SHOPPING LIST

1 lb	package phyllo dough
1 cup	unsalted butter
	For the nut filling
2 cups	shelled unsalted pistachio nuts
2 cups	walnut pieces
¼ cup	sugar
2 tsp	ground cinnamon
1	large pinch of ground cloves
	For the honey syrup
1 cup	sugar
1 cup	water
1 cup	honey
1	lemon
3 tbsp	orange-flower water

ORDER OF WORK

1 PREPARE THE NUT FILLING

2 ASSEMBLE AND BAKE THE PASTRIES

3 MAKE THE HONEY SYRUP

4 FINISH THE PASTRIES

1 PREPARE THE NUT FILLING

1 Coarsely chop the pistachio nuts with the chef's knife or in a food processor, and then chop the walnuts.

2 Set aside 3–4 tbsp of the chopped pistachios for decoration; put the remainder in a medium bowl with the chopped walnuts, sugar, cinnamon, and cloves. Stir to combine.

Pistachio nuts add hint of color to filling

2 ASSEMBLE AND BAKE THE PASTRIES

1 Heat the oven to 350°F. Lay a dish towel on a work surface and sprinkle it lightly with water. Unroll the phyllo dough sheets on the towel and cover them with a second dampened towel to prevent them drying out.

Be sure to sprinkle filling right up to edge of pan

2 Melt the butter in a small saucepan. Brush the baking pan with a little melted butter. Take 1 sheet of phyllo dough and line the pan with it, folding over one end to fit.

! TAKE CARE !
Do not allow the phyllo to dry out or it will be difficult to handle. Work with 1 sheet at a time, keeping the rest covered.

3 Brush the dough with melted butter and gently press it into the corners and sides of the pan. Lay another sheet of dough on top, brush with butter, and press it into the pan as before. Continue layering the dough, buttering each sheet, until one-third has been used. Scatter half the nut filling over the dough.

If butter begins to harden, melt it again over low heat

ANNE SAYS
"Butter the sheets as lightly and evenly as possible."

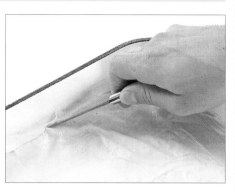

4 Layer another third of the phyllo sheets in the pan, buttering each one and pressing into the corners and sides as before, then sprinkle the remaining nut filling on top.

5 Layer the remaining phyllo sheets, buttering them and pressing them into the pan as before. Trim off excess dough with the small knife. Brush the top sheet of dough thoroughly with butter and pour any remaining butter over the top.

6 With the small knife, cut diagonal lines ½ inch deep in the layered pastry, to mark out 1½-inch diamond shapes. Do not press down on the layered pastry when cutting.

7 Bake on a low shelf in the heated oven until golden, 1¼–1½ hours. The skewer inserted in the center should be hot to the touch when withdrawn after 30 seconds. Meanwhile, make the syrup.

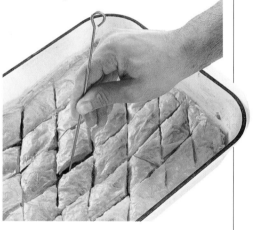

3 MAKE THE HONEY SYRUP

1 Put the sugar and water in a medium saucepan and heat until dissolved, stirring occasionally. Pour in the honey and stir to mix. Boil without stirring until the syrup reaches the soft ball stage, 239°F on the candy thermometer, about 25 minutes.

ANNE SAYS
"To test the syrup without a thermometer, take the pan from the heat and dip a teaspoon in the hot syrup. Let the syrup cool a few seconds, then take a little between your finger and thumb; it should form a soft ball."

Clear honey makes sparkling syrup

2 Remove the syrup from the heat and let cool to lukewarm. Squeeze the juice from the lemon and add it to the syrup. Stir in the orange-flower water or 1 tsp vanilla extract.

4 FINISH THE PASTRIES

For maximum absorption, pour syrup over pastries while they are still hot

1 Remove the baking pan from the oven and immediately pour the cool syrup evenly over the hot pastries. With the chef's knife, cut along the marked lines in the pastry, almost to the bottom of the pan, then let the pastries cool.

ANNE SAYS
"*This process allows the honey syrup to penetrate the bottom pastry layers.*"

¶◎¶ TO SERVE
Cut through the marked lines completely. Carefully lift out the pastries with the metal spatula and arrange them on each dessert plate. Sprinkle the top of each pastry with the reserved chopped pistachio nuts.

Nut and honey pastries are popular throughout the Middle East

Diamond-shaped pastries look appealing

VARIATION
PHYLLO NUT ROLLS
In this variation of Baklava, the delicious nut filling is rolled pinwheel-style between sheets of phyllo dough.

1 Make the nut filling as directed in the main recipe, using all of the pistachio nuts.
2 Cut the phyllo dough into 24 sheets, each measuring 9 x 5 inches. Keep them covered with a damp dish towel to prevent them drying out.
3 Lay 1 piece of dough flat on the work surface, fold it crosswise in half, and brush it with melted butter. Spread 1–2 tbsp of the nut filling evenly on the dough, leaving a 1/2-inch border. Fold in 2 opposite borders (this prevents filling from spilling out). From the nearest open edge, roll up the dough neatly but loosely into a cylinder.
4 Set the roll, seam-side down, in the buttered baking pan. Continue until all the dough and filling have been used. Pack the rolls loosely in the baking pan to fill it completely.
5 Brush the phyllo nut rolls with the remaining melted butter. Bake them in the heated oven until crisp and golden brown, 30–40 minutes.
6 Meanwhile, make the honey syrup as directed.
7 Pour the cold syrup over the hot pastry rolls and let cool.

ORANGE AND CINNAMON CREME BRULEE

¶O¶ SERVES 8 ⊌ WORK TIME 15–20 MINUTES* ♨ BAKING TIME 30–35 MINUTES

EQUIPMENT

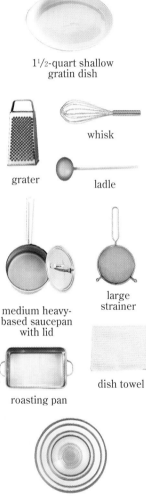

1½-quart shallow gratin dish

whisk

grater

ladle

medium heavy-based saucepan with lid

large strainer

roasting pan

dish towel

bowls

small strainer

In this dessert, translated as burnt cream, a rich custard is sprinkled with sugar just before serving, then broiled to form a golden layer of caramel. The topping will crack when tapped with a spoon, adding a crisp dimension, while cinnamon and orange give complexity to the satin-smooth baked cream. Fresh berries or a compote of peaches would make a perfect accompaniment to the crème brûlée.

GETTING AHEAD

The orange-cinnamon cream can be baked up to 8 hours ahead and kept refrigerated. Caramelize the sugar not more than 2 hours before serving.

* plus 3–8 hours chilling time

SHOPPING LIST

1		orange
1		cinnamon stick
1 quart		heavy cream
8		egg yolks
1 cup		sugar

INGREDIENTS

orange

cinnamon stick

heavy cream

sugar

egg yolks

ORDER OF WORK

1 MAKE THE ORANGE-CINNAMON CREAM

2 CARAMELIZE THE CREAM

1 MAKE THE ORANGE-CINNAMON CREAM

1 Heat the oven to 375°F. Using the coarse grid of the grater, grate the zest from the orange, avoiding white pith.

2 Snap the cinnamon stick in half and place in the saucepan. Warm the saucepan over low heat until you can smell the spice, 40–60 seconds.

3 Let the saucepan cool slightly, then add the cream and the grated orange zest to the cinnamon. Bring the cream just to a boil.

Whisk egg yolks only just until mixed, so custard is not too frothy

4 Remove the pan from the heat, cover with the lid, and let the cream infuse, 10–15 minutes.

5 Put the egg yolks and one-third of the sugar in a large bowl. Whisk together just until mixed.

6 Slowly pour the cream mixture into the egg yolks, whisking constantly until evenly mixed.

7 Ladle the cream mixture through the large strainer into the gratin dish. Fold the dish towel and put it on the bottom of the roasting pan; set the gratin dish on the towel.

Orange zest and pieces of cinnamon are strained out of cream

8 Pour enough hot water into the roasting pan to come about halfway up the sides of the dish. Bring the water bath to a boil on top of the stove, then carefully transfer the water bath to the heated oven.

When testing if custard is cooked, move dish carefully so skin is not broken

9 Bake the cream until a thin skin forms on top and the cream underneath is almost firm when the dish is gently moved from side to side, 30–35 minutes. Remove the dish from the roasting pan and let cool to room temperature. Chill, 3–8 hours.

2 CARAMELIZE THE CREAM

1 Heat the broiler. Sprinkle the surface of the orange-cinnamon cream with the remaining sugar to form a thin, even layer.

! TAKE CARE !
Wipe off any sugar from the edge of the dish because it will burn under the broiler.

Sprinkle sugar through small strainer to ensure surface is evenly covered, right to side of dish

2 Half-fill the roasting pan with cold water and set the gratin dish in it. Add some ice cubes to the water.

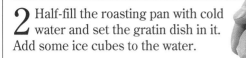

Ice water keeps cream cold so it does not overcook under broiler

3 Broil the cream as close to the heat as possible until the sugar melts and caramelizes all over, 2–3 minutes. Let cool a few minutes so the caramel becomes crisp.

ANNE SAYS
"It is essential that the sugar is cooked under very high heat so it caramelizes before the cream overcooks. The broiler must be at maximum heat."

🍴 **TO SERVE**
Crack the caramel with the back of a spoon to reach the orange-cinnamon cream beneath.

Caramel will remain crisp 2–3 hours

Smooth cream is lightly spiced with cinnamon and orange

V A R I A T I O N

LEMON CREME BRULEE WITH BLACKBERRIES

Here, tart blackberries are layered under a soft lemon cream, providing an ingenious contrast of color, taste, and texture.

1 Omit the cinnamon. Make the cream mixture as directed, using the coarsely grated zest of 1 lemon instead of 1 orange.
2 Pick over 2 pints blackberries, washing them only if they are dirty. Divide the blackberries among 8 ramekins, each 1-cup capacity, scattering the berries to form a single layer. Fill the dishes with the lemon cream mixture.
3 Bake the creams in a water bath in the heated oven, 15–20 minutes. Caramelize them as directed.
4 Serve with extra blackberries, if you like.

CHOCOLATE DECADENCE WITH RASPBERRY COULIS

🍽 SERVES 8   🥣 WORK TIME 30–40 MINUTES*   🍲 BAKING TIME 20 MINUTES

EQUIPMENT

9-inch round cake pan with sloping sides

chef's knife

whisk †

large metal spoon

small ladle

pastry brush

food processor

small knife

metal bowl

strainer

2 wire racks

bowls

rubber spatula

wooden spoon

saucepan

scissors

parchment paper

serrated knife

† electric mixer can also be used

Rich and dense, this cake relies wholly on melted chocolate, butter, and eggs, with only 2 tablespoons of sugar and 1 tablespoon of flour. It is served with a fresh raspberry coulis to cut the richness, and a light touch of whipped cream.

GETTING AHEAD

The cake can be stored up to 1 week in an airtight container, and it freezes well. Prepare the raspberry coulis 1 day ahead, and store it, in a covered bowl, in the refrigerator. Whip the cream not more than 2 hours before serving.

* plus 2 hours chilling time

SHOPPING LIST

1 lb	semisweet chocolate
²⁄₃ cup	unsalted butter, more for cake pan
6	eggs
2 tbsp	granulated sugar
1 tbsp	flour, more for cake pan
	For the raspberry coulis
1¹⁄₂ pints	raspberries
2–3 tbsp	confectioners' sugar
	For the decoration
1¹⁄₂ cups	heavy cream
1¹⁄₂ tbsp	granulated sugar
¹⁄₂ cup	raspberries
8	small sprigs of fresh mint

INGREDIENTS

semisweet chocolate

raspberries †

granulated sugar

heavy cream

flour

unsalted butter

fresh mint

eggs

confectioners' sugar

† defrosted raspberries can be used for the coulis

ORDER OF WORK

1   MAKE THE CHOCOLATE CAKE

2   PREPARE THE RASPBERRY COULIS AND WHIPPED CREAM

3   DECORATE THE CAKE

1 MAKE THE CHOCOLATE CAKE

1 Heat the oven to 400°F. Fold a square of parchment paper into quarters, then fold it again into eighths to form a narrow triangle. Hold the point of the paper triangle over the center of the cake pan base and cut the paper even with the edge.

2 Brush the pan with melted butter. Unfold the paper and press it onto the bottom of the pan. Butter the paper. Sprinkle in 2–3 tbsp flour, then turn and shake the pan so that the flour evenly coats the bottom and side. Tap the pan to remove all excess flour.

3 Cut the chocolate into large chunks. Coarsely chop the chunks in the food processor using the pulse button. Alternatively, you can chop them on a chopping board with the chef's knife.

Water bath helps prevent chocolate burning

4 Cut the butter into pieces and put them in a large heatproof bowl with the chopped chocolate. Set the bowl over a pan of hot, but not simmering, water (a water bath). Stir until the mixture is melted and smooth. Remove the bowl from the pan of hot water and let cool, stirring occasionally.

5 Separate the eggs. Beat the egg yolks into the chocolate mixture with the wooden spoon.

Whisked egg whites should hold stiff peaks

6 Put the egg whites in the metal bowl and beat with the whisk or electric mixer until stiff. Add the sugar; continue whisking until glossy to make a light meringue, about 20 seconds.

7 Stir the flour into the chocolate mixture; fold in one-third of the egg whites to lighten it: cut down into the center of the bowl with the rubber spatula, scoop under the contents, and turn them over in a rolling motion. At the same time, with the other hand, slowly turn the bowl counter-clockwise. Fold in the remaining whisked egg whites in 2 batches.

8 Transfer the batter to the prepared cake pan. Tap it on the work surface to level the batter and knock out any air bubbles. Bake in the heated oven until crusty on top but still soft in the center, about 20 minutes. Let the cake cool completely in the pan, set on a wire rack. When cold, chill, 2 hours.

Scrape mixture from bowl with rubber spatula

9 To unmold the cake, place a wire rack on top of the pan and turn both over together. If the cake sticks to the pan, loosen it by warming the pan briefly in hot water. Lift off the pan, and peel the lining paper from the base of the cake. Set the second wire rack on the cake and turn both over so the cake is base down on the rack.

2 PREPARE THE RASPBERRY COULIS AND WHIPPED CREAM

Fresh raspberries are plump and firm

1 Make the raspberry coulis: pick over the raspberries, washing them only if they are dirty.

2 Put the raspberries in the food processor or a blender. Work the berries in the machine until they are puréed. Add confectioners' sugar to taste. Purée again until the sugar is evenly blended.

Remove seeds for smooth coulis

3 Work the puréed raspberries through the strainer into a bowl to remove the seeds.

4 Pour 1¼ cups of the cream into a chilled bowl and whip until soft peaks form. Add the granulated sugar and continue whipping until stiff peaks form. Cover the bowl, and chill until ready to serve.

3 DECORATE THE CAKE

1 Using the serrated knife, cut the cake into 8 wedges. Set 1 wedge in the center of each dessert plate.

ANNE SAYS
"Dipping the knife in hot water makes it easy to cut neat wedges."

3 Dip the tip of the small knife into the remaining cream and drizzle a curved line on the coulis. Pull the tip of the knife across the cream to make a feathered design.

Pale cream contrasts with red coulis

2 Ladle a small pool of raspberry coulis onto each plate near the tip of the wedge of cake.

🍽 **TO SERVE**
Place a spoonful of whipped cream next to the cake and decorate with a few whole raspberries and a mint sprig.

Triangle of chocolate cake looks rich and elegant

Raspberry coulis is a delicious partner for chocolate

V A R I A T I O N

CHOCOLATE DECADENCE WITH PASSION FRUIT SAUCE

Here, a passion fruit sauce balances the richness of the chocolate cake. If passion fruit are not available, substitute 2 ripe mangoes.

1 Omit the raspberries and mint sprigs. Make the cake as directed.
2 Make a passion fruit sauce: halve 18–20 passion fruit (total weight about 1¹/₂ lb) and scrape the pulp and seeds into a fine strainer set over a bowl. With a wooden spoon, rub the pulp through the strainer, then discard the seeds. Beat 4–5 tbsp confectioners' sugar into the passion fruit pulp and taste, adding more sugar if needed. Chill the passion fruit sauce until ready to serve.
3 Prepare the whipped cream as directed, and chill.
4 Serve the cake as directed, on a pool of passion fruit sauce. Pipe a rosette of whipped cream on each slice of cake.

GINGER CHEESECAKE

🍽 SERVES 8–10   🥄 WORK TIME 40–45 MINUTES*   🍲 BAKING TIME 50–60 MINUTES

EQUIPMENT

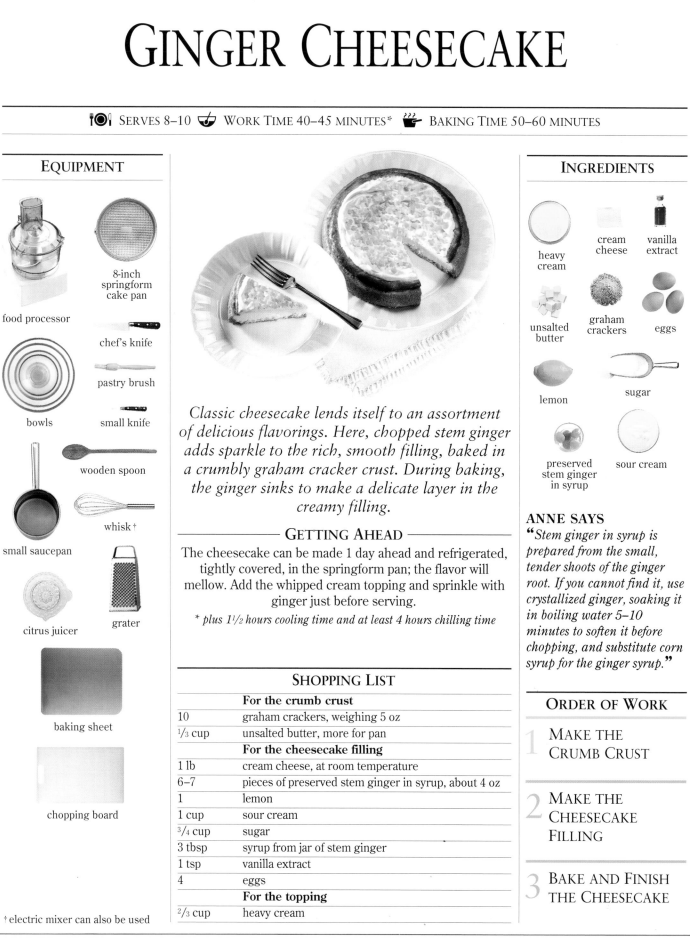

food processor

8-inch springform cake pan

chef's knife

pastry brush

bowls

small knife

wooden spoon

whisk †

small saucepan

citrus juicer

grater

baking sheet

chopping board

† electric mixer can also be used

INGREDIENTS

heavy cream

cream cheese

vanilla extract

unsalted butter

graham crackers

eggs

lemon

sugar

preserved stem ginger in syrup

sour cream

Classic cheesecake lends itself to an assortment of delicious flavorings. Here, chopped stem ginger adds sparkle to the rich, smooth filling, baked in a crumbly graham cracker crust. During baking, the ginger sinks to make a delicate layer in the creamy filling.

GETTING AHEAD
The cheesecake can be made 1 day ahead and refrigerated, tightly covered, in the springform pan; the flavor will mellow. Add the whipped cream topping and sprinkle with ginger just before serving.

* plus 1½ hours cooling time and at least 4 hours chilling time

ANNE SAYS
"*Stem ginger in syrup is prepared from the small, tender shoots of the ginger root. If you cannot find it, use crystallized ginger, soaking it in boiling water 5–10 minutes to soften it before chopping, and substitute corn syrup for the ginger syrup.*"

ORDER OF WORK

1 MAKE THE CRUMB CRUST

2 MAKE THE CHEESECAKE FILLING

3 BAKE AND FINISH THE CHEESECAKE

SHOPPING LIST

	For the crumb crust
10	graham crackers, weighing 5 oz
⅓ cup	unsalted butter, more for pan
	For the cheesecake filling
1 lb	cream cheese, at room temperature
6–7	pieces of preserved stem ginger in syrup, about 4 oz
1	lemon
1 cup	sour cream
¾ cup	sugar
3 tbsp	syrup from jar of stem ginger
1 tsp	vanilla extract
4	eggs
	For the topping
⅔ cup	heavy cream

1 MAKE THE CRUMB CRUST

1 Generously butter the bottom and side of the springform pan, then chill it to set the butter.

2 Work the graham crackers in the food processor to form fine crumbs; you should have 1¹/₂ cups. Put them in a bowl.

ANNE SAYS
"Alternatively, you can put the graham crackers in a plastic bag and crush them with a rolling pin."

3 Melt the butter in the saucepan and add it to the crumbs. Stir together with the wooden spoon until all the crumbs are moistened with melted butter.

Spread crumbs evenly before pressing them down

4 Press the crumb mixture evenly over the bottom and 1¹/₂ inches up the side of the prepared pan. Chill until firm, 30–60 minutes. Meanwhile, make the cheesecake filling.

2 MAKE THE CHEESECAKE FILLING

1 Using the wooden spoon, beat the cream cheese in a bowl until soft and smooth.

Syrup from ginger is used in filling

2 With the chef's knife, chop the stem ginger. Reserve 2 tbsp of the ginger for the topping. Finely grate the zest from the lemon and squeeze 2 tsp juice.

3 Add the remaining chopped ginger, the sour cream, sugar, ginger syrup, vanilla extract, and lemon zest and juice to the cream cheese, and beat just until smooth.

Chunks of ginger add texture to filling

4 Add the eggs, one at a time, to the cream cheese and ginger mixture, beating well after each addition.

3 BAKE AND FINISH THE CHEESECAKE

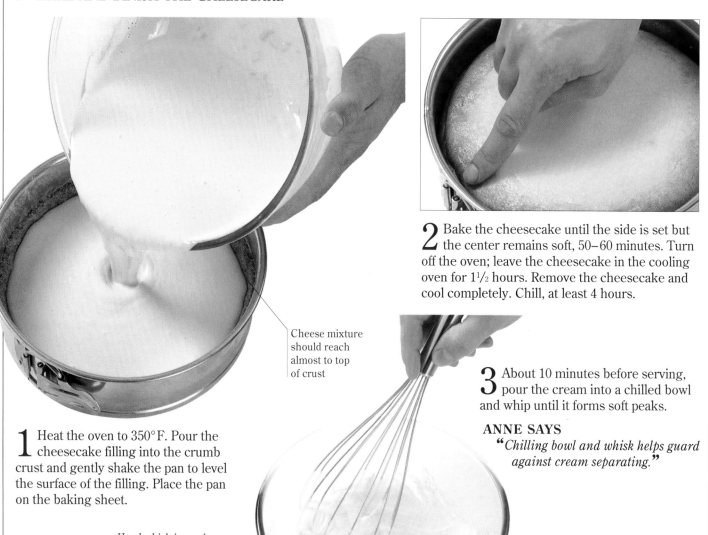

Cheese mixture should reach almost to top of crust

Hand whisk is used here but electric mixer can also be used

1 Heat the oven to 350°F. Pour the cheesecake filling into the crumb crust and gently shake the pan to level the surface of the filling. Place the pan on the baking sheet.

2 Bake the cheesecake until the side is set but the center remains soft, 50–60 minutes. Turn off the oven; leave the cheesecake in the cooling oven for 1½ hours. Remove the cheesecake and cool completely. Chill, at least 4 hours.

3 About 10 minutes before serving, pour the cream into a chilled bowl and whip until it forms soft peaks.

ANNE SAYS
"Chilling bowl and whisk helps guard against cream separating."

Cream should
hold soft peaks

4 Run the small knife around the cheesecake to loosen it, then remove the pan side. Transfer the cheesecake to a serving plate. Swirl the whipped cream over the top.

5 Sprinkle the reserved chopped stem ginger evenly over the whipped cream topping.

Preserved ginger
gives cheesecake a
piquant bite

🍴 **TO SERVE**
Cut the cheesecake into wedges and serve on dessert plates.

**Graham cracker
crumb crust** is
traditional for
cheesecake

SOUR CREAM AND FRUIT CHEESECAKE

A smooth topping of sour cream contrasts with the bright fruit that decorates this cheesecake, while the filling is accented with lemon juice and zest.

1 Omit the stem ginger, ginger syrup, and heavy cream for the topping. Make the crumb crust as directed; press into the springform cake pan.
2 Make the cheesecake filling as directed, using all the juice from the lemon. Bake, cool, and chill the cheesecake as directed.
3 Spread 1 cup sour cream evenly over the top of the cold cheesecake.
4 Arrange mixed fresh berries (for example, blueberries and red currants) decoratively on top of the cheesecake, and arrange more fruit and fresh mint sprigs on the plate. Serve with additional berries, if you like.

35

SPANISH ROLLED SPONGE CAKE

🍽 SERVES 8–10 🥄 WORK TIME 40–45 MINUTES* 🍲 BAKING TIME 7–9 MINUTES

EQUIPMENT

metal bowl

chef's knife

small knife

whisk

pastry brush

metal spatula

strainers

electric mixer

vegetable peeler

wooden spoon

grater

2 baking sheets, each 12 x 14 inches

dish towel

bowls

parchment paper

rubber spatula

serrated knife

saucepans

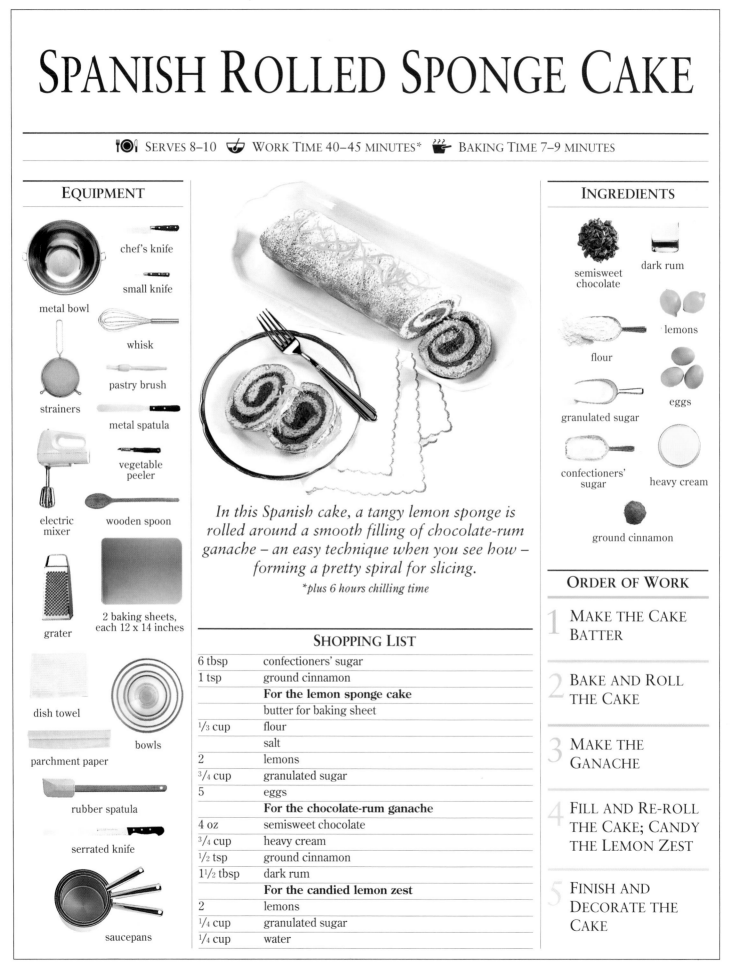

In this Spanish cake, a tangy lemon sponge is rolled around a smooth filling of chocolate-rum ganache – an easy technique when you see how – forming a pretty spiral for slicing.

plus 6 hours chilling time

SHOPPING LIST

6 tbsp	confectioners' sugar
1 tsp	ground cinnamon
	For the lemon sponge cake
	butter for baking sheet
1/3 cup	flour
	salt
2	lemons
3/4 cup	granulated sugar
5	eggs
	For the chocolate-rum ganache
4 oz	semisweet chocolate
3/4 cup	heavy cream
1/2 tsp	ground cinnamon
1 1/2 tbsp	dark rum
	For the candied lemon zest
2	lemons
1/4 cup	granulated sugar
1/4 cup	water

INGREDIENTS

semisweet chocolate

dark rum

lemons

flour

eggs

granulated sugar

confectioners' sugar

heavy cream

ground cinnamon

ORDER OF WORK

1 MAKE THE CAKE BATTER

2 BAKE AND ROLL THE CAKE

3 MAKE THE GANACHE

4 FILL AND RE-ROLL THE CAKE; CANDY THE LEMON ZEST

5 FINISH AND DECORATE THE CAKE

36

1 MAKE THE CAKE BATTER

1 Heat the oven to 425°F. Brush 1 baking sheet with butter, line it with parchment, and butter the paper.

2 Sift the flour with a pinch of salt. Finely grate the lemon zest into a large bowl. Add two-thirds of the sugar. Separate the eggs and add the yolks to the sugar and lemon zest.

Lemon zest should be finely grated to mix evenly in batter

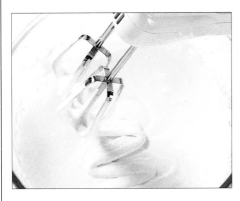

3 With the electric mixer or whisk, beat the egg yolks, sugar, and lemon zest until pale and the mixture leaves a ribbon trail when the beaters are lifted, 3–5 minutes.

4 In the metal bowl, whisk the egg whites until stiff. Sprinkle in the remaining sugar and whisk until glossy to make a light meringue, about 20 seconds.

ANNE SAYS
"Your bowl and whisk must be completely free of any trace of water or grease, or the egg whites will not whisk to full volume."

Flour and meringue are folded in in 3 batches

5 Sift about one-third of the flour over the egg yolk mixture. Add about one-third of the meringue.

6 Fold the mixtures together: cut down into the center with the rubber spatula, scoop under the contents, and turn them over in a rolling motion. At the same time, turn the bowl counter-clockwise. Continue folding until the mixtures are well blended. Fold in the remaining flour and meringue in 2 batches.

2 BAKE AND ROLL THE CAKE

Cover baking
sheet evenly
with cake batter

1 Pour the cake
batter onto the
prepared baking sheet and
spread it evenly almost to the
edges, using the metal spatula.

2 Bake toward the bottom of the
heated oven until the cake has
risen, is just firm to the touch, and is
golden brown, 7–9 minutes.

! TAKE CARE !
*Do not overbake the cake or it will be
difficult to roll.*

3 Remove the cake from
the oven and cover it
immediately with a
dampened dish towel.

ANNE SAYS
*"The damp towel keeps the
cake moist and pliable."*

Lay towel gently
on cake to cover
it completely

Towel should be
damp but not wet

4 Take the second baking sheet and
set it on top of the towel. Quickly
invert so the original baking sheet is on
top. Carefully remove the uppermost
baking sheet.

5 Holding the parchment paper
lining at one corner, carefully peel
it off the cake and discard.

6 With a short side of the cake nearest to you, fold the end of the towel over the cake, then tightly roll up the cake. Let cool completely.

Towel separates rolled layers of cake to prevent them sticking

3 MAKE THE GANACHE

1 Cut the chocolate into large chunks. Coarsely chop them with the chef's knife, or in a food processor using the pulse button. Put the chocolate in a large bowl.

2 Heat the cream with the cinnamon in a small saucepan until almost boiling. Add to the chopped chocolate and stir until the chocolate has melted. Let cool, stirring occasionally.

3 Add the rum. Using the electric mixer, beat the ganache until it becomes thick and fluffy, 5–10 minutes.

! TAKE CARE !
Do not overbeat the ganache or it will be very stiff and hard to spread.

HOW TO MAKE CANDIED LEMON ZEST

Candied lemon zest adds flavor to creamy desserts as well as being an attractive decoration.

1 Thinly pare the zest from the lemons with a vegetable peeler, and cut it into fine julienne strips with a knife. Alternatively, shave strips of zest from the lemons using a citrus zester. Add the strips to a small saucepan of boiling water. Simmer 2 minutes, then drain.

2 Gently heat the sugar and the ¼ cup water in the saucepan until dissolved. Add the strips of zest and simmer until the zest is translucent, 8–10 minutes.

3 Remove the zest with a fork and spread it on a sheet of parchment paper to cool.

4 FILL AND RE-ROLL THE CAKE; CANDY THE LEMON ZEST

Pull cake gently
when unrolling

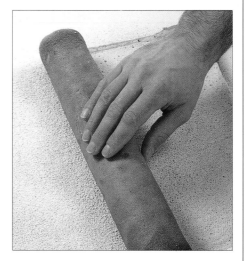

1 Holding the towel steady with one hand, unroll the cooled cake with the other hand. Then re-roll the cake without the towel.

2 Combine half of the confectioners' sugar with the cinnamon in a small strainer. Sprinkle the mixture evenly over a large sheet of parchment paper. Place the cake on the sugared paper and unroll it.

3 Using the metal spatula, spread the chocolate-rum ganache evenly over the cake. Trim the short edges to remove the crust.

Sugar-cinnamon coating
will be on outside of
finished cake

Ensuring cake is
tightly rolled will
make it easier
to slice

5 Bring the paper up over the cake and fold it in tightly. Insert the edge of the baking sheet against the fold and push away from you to tighten the roll.

ANNE SAYS
"This shapes the roll evenly."

4 Starting at the same short end, carefully roll up the filled cake as tightly as possible, lifting it with the parchment paper.

ANNE SAYS
"If necessary, tape the twisted ends of the paper package to be sure they remain tightly sealed."

Wrap rolled cake tightly for storage in the refrigerator

6 Twist the ends of the paper to seal. Chill the cake until the ganache filling is firm, at least 6 hours. Meanwhile, make the candied lemon zest (see box, page 39).

5 FINISH AND DECORATE THE CAKE

1 Unwrap the cake. With the serrated knife, trim each end of the cake, cutting on the diagonal. Sift the remaining confectioners' sugar over the cake and scatter the candied lemon zest along the top. Transfer the cake to a serving plate. Cut the cake across into 3/4-inch slices to serve.

Candied lemon zest forms a brightly colored decoration

Sprinkle even coating of sugar over cake

— **GETTING AHEAD** —
Once assembled, the cake can be kept, tightly covered, 1–2 days in the refrigerator. Decorate just before serving.

VARIATION

INDIVIDUAL SPONGE CAKE ROLLS

The delicate shape of these individual sponge rolls is instantly appealing. As a simple decoration, each end is dipped in grated chocolate.

1 Omit the candied lemon zest and cinnamon. Make, roll, and cool the sponge cake as directed.
2 Make the ganache as directed.
3 After unrolling the cake on the sheet of sugared paper, cut it crosswise in half. Spread the ganache over both pieces of cake, then roll up each one separately, starting at a long edge. Tighten the rolls with the paper and baking sheet as directed, then wrap and chill as directed.
4 Just before serving, cut each rolled sponge cake on the diagonal with the serrated knife into 4 portions, discarding the ends.
5 Holding a 1 oz piece of semisweet chocolate in a piece of parchment paper or foil, work it against the largest grid of a grater to obtain coarse chocolate shavings.
6 Melt 2 tbsp apricot jam in a small saucepan. Dip a pastry brush in the jam and brush it on the ends of each of the 8 cake rolls, then dip them in the chocolate shavings. Sprinkle the rolls with confectioners' sugar and top with a little more grated chocolate, then serve on a large platter. Serves 8.

HAZELNUT MERINGUE GATEAU

Dacquoise

🍽 SERVES 6–8   🥄 WORK TIME 50–60 MINUTES*   🍲 BAKING TIME 40–50 MINUTES

EQUIPMENT

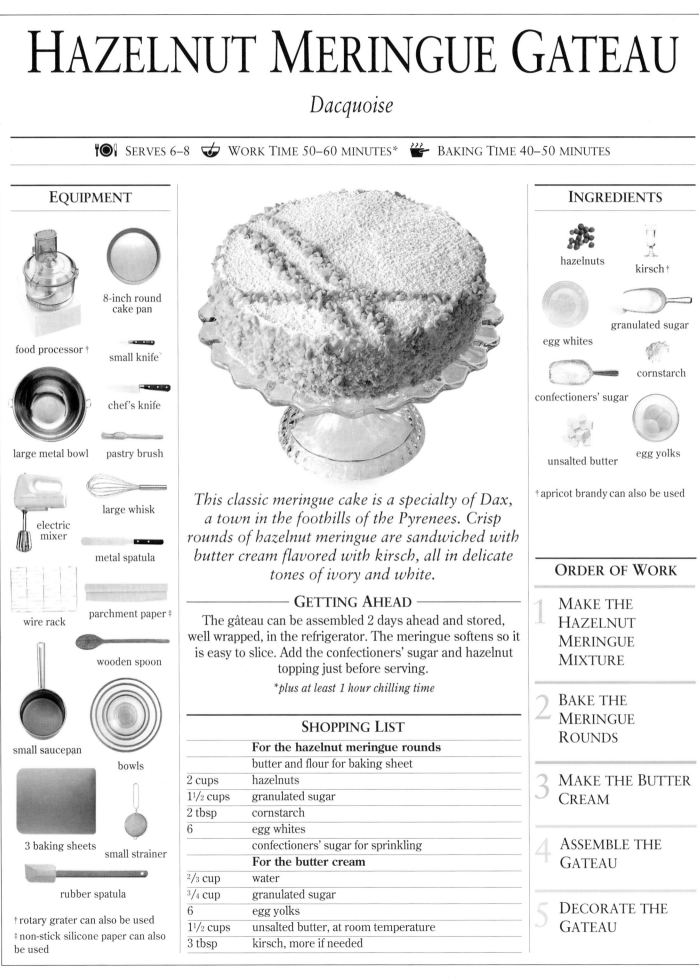

8-inch round cake pan

food processor †

small knife

chef's knife

large metal bowl

pastry brush

large whisk

electric mixer

metal spatula

wire rack

parchment paper ‡

wooden spoon

small saucepan

bowls

3 baking sheets

small strainer

rubber spatula

† rotary grater can also be used
‡ non-stick silicone paper can also be used

INGREDIENTS

hazelnuts

kirsch †

granulated sugar

egg whites

cornstarch

confectioners' sugar

unsalted butter

egg yolks

† apricot brandy can also be used

This classic meringue cake is a specialty of Dax, a town in the foothills of the Pyrenees. Crisp rounds of hazelnut meringue are sandwiched with butter cream flavored with kirsch, all in delicate tones of ivory and white.

GETTING AHEAD

The gâteau can be assembled 2 days ahead and stored, well wrapped, in the refrigerator. The meringue softens so it is easy to slice. Add the confectioners' sugar and hazelnut topping just before serving.

*plus at least 1 hour chilling time

SHOPPING LIST

	For the hazelnut meringue rounds	
	butter and flour for baking sheet	
2 cups	hazelnuts	
1½ cups	granulated sugar	
2 tbsp	cornstarch	
6	egg whites	
	confectioners' sugar for sprinkling	
	For the butter cream	
²/₃ cup	water	
³/₄ cup	granulated sugar	
6	egg yolks	
1½ cups	unsalted butter, at room temperature	
3 tbsp	kirsch, more if needed	

ORDER OF WORK

1 MAKE THE HAZELNUT MERINGUE MIXTURE

2 BAKE THE MERINGUE ROUNDS

3 MAKE THE BUTTER CREAM

4 ASSEMBLE THE GATEAU

5 DECORATE THE GATEAU

1 MAKE THE HAZELNUT MERINGUE MIXTURE

1 Brush the baking sheets with melted butter and line them with parchment paper. Butter the paper and sprinkle it with flour, discarding the excess. With your finger, trace 1 circle on each baking sheet, using the upturned cake pan as a guide.

ANNE SAYS
"If you do not have 3 baking sheets, you can use the base of an upturned roasting pan to bake the meringue rounds."

Upturned cake pan makes accurate guide

HOW TO TOAST AND SKIN NUTS

Toasting nuts intensifies their flavor. It also makes it easier to remove thin skin from nuts such as hazelnuts. You can tell that they are toasted when the skins start to pop and the nuts smell fragrant.

1 Heat the oven to 350°F. Spread out the nuts on a baking sheet and bake until lightly browned, 6–15 minutes depending on the type of nut and if they are whole or chopped. Stir occasionally during baking so they color evenly.

2 Toast the hazelnuts in the oven 12–15 minutes, then skin them (see box, right). Reserve about one-third of the hazelnuts for decoration. Put half of the granulated sugar, together with the remaining hazelnuts, in the food processor.

3 Process until the mixture is quite fine. Alternatively, grind the nuts by themselves, using a rotary grater.

! TAKE CARE !
Do not overwork the nuts or they will release their oil, creating a paste. Grinding with sugar helps prevent this.

4 Transfer the ground hazelnuts and sugar to a medium bowl and stir in the cornstarch.

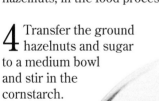

Cornstarch absorbs moisture, making meringue crisp and dry

2 To remove the skins from hazelnuts: quickly rub the toasted nuts in a rough dish towel while they are still hot. Discard the skins and leave the nuts to cool.

Fold in nut mixture
gently so meringue
stays light

6 Add one-third of the
hazelnut mixture to the
meringue and fold the
mixtures together as lightly
as possible with the rubber
spatula: cut down into the center
of the bowl, scoop under the
contents, and turn them over in a
rolling motion. At the same time, with
your other hand, turn the bowl counter-
clockwise. Fold in the remaining
hazelnut mixture in 2 batches.

5 Put the egg whites in the metal
bowl. Beat with the whisk or
electric mixer until stiff peaks form.
Sprinkle in the remaining granulated
sugar and continue whisking until
glossy to make a light meringue,
about 20 seconds.

Rubber spatula
is best utensil
for folding

2 BAKE THE MERINGUE ROUNDS

1 Heat the oven to 250°F. Divide the
hazelnut meringue evenly among
the circles and spread it out with the
metal spatula inside the marked lines
to make 3 even, flat disks.

ANNE SAYS
*"Alternatively, you can pipe the
meringue disks. Use a ⅝-inch
plain tube and pipe the meringue
in spirals,
starting in the
center of each
circle."*

Spread meringue
evenly to fill
marked circle

2 Bake the hazelnut meringue
rounds in the heated oven, rotating
the baking sheets occasionally, until
the rounds are all lightly browned and
feel dry to the touch, 40–50 minutes.

3 Remove the baking sheets from the
oven. While the meringue is still
warm, trim the edges with the small
knife, using the cake pan as a guide.
Carefully peel off the paper, transfer
the meringue rounds to the wire rack,
and let cool.

Rest hand lightly
on cake pan so
meringue is not
crushed

3 MAKE THE BUTTER CREAM

1 Put the water and granulated sugar in the saucepan and heat until dissolved. Boil the syrup without stirring until it reaches the soft ball stage. To test, take the pan from the heat, dip a teaspoon in the hot syrup, remove, and let cool a few seconds. Take a little syrup between your finger and thumb; it should form a soft ball.

ANNE SAYS
"You can also test the syrup with a candy thermometer; it should register 239°F."

Stir sugar and water only once before heating so syrup does not crystallize

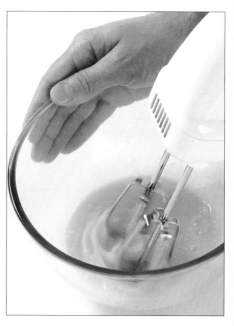

2 While the sugar syrup is boiling, beat the egg yolks in a large bowl, just until they are mixed.

Move mixer around bowl to ensure all butter is creamed

Butter will become light and fluffy as you beat

3 Gradually pour the hot sugar syrup into the egg yolks in a steady stream, beating constantly.

4 Continue beating at high speed until the mixture is cool and forms a thick mousse, about 5 minutes.

5 Put the butter in a medium bowl and beat it with the electric mixer or the wooden spoon until it is smooth and creamy.

6 Gradually add the butter to the cool egg mousse and beat to combine.

ANNE SAYS
"Be sure the egg mousse has cooled or it will melt the butter."

Creamed butter quickly disperses in egg mousse

7 Beat the 3 tbsp kirsch into the egg mousse and butter mixture, adding more kirsch to taste, if necessary.

4 ASSEMBLE THE GATEAU

1 Cut a round of cardboard to fit the gâteau. Add a dab of butter cream, set 1 meringue round on the cardboard, and press lightly so it sticks. Place the cardboard on the upturned cake pan to raise it off the work surface, if you like.

2 Spoon about one-quarter of the butter cream onto the meringue and spread with the metal spatula to cover the meringue evenly. Place a second meringue round on top and spread it with another quarter of the butter cream.

Use cardboard to turn gâteau as you spread butter cream around side

Spread butter cream gently to avoid crushing meringue

3 Cover with the third meringue round. Spread the remaining butter cream over the whole gâteau so that it is completely covered.

Cardboard supports meringue rounds so they are easy to handle

5 DECORATE THE GATEAU

1 Using the small strainer, cover the top of the gâteau thickly with sifted confectioners' sugar.

2 Using the chef's knife, finely chop the reserved hazelnuts. Press most of the hazelnuts around the side of the gâteau, using your hands.

3 Arrange the remaining hazelnuts on top of the gâteau in neat lines, using the edge of the chef's knife. Chill until firm, at least 1 hour.

Hold knife at shallow angle when placing nuts on the cake

🍽 TO SERVE
Transfer the gâteau to a flat cake stand or serving plate, lined with a paper doily if you like. Cut the gâteau into wedges for serving.

Meringue gâteau is best served lightly chilled so butter cream is firm

Crunchy hazelnut decoration contrasts with butter cream filling

ALMOND MERINGUE GATEAU

Armagnac-flavored butter cream and meringue made with toasted almonds combine in a punchy version of classic Dacquoise. This gâteau originated near the Armagnac region of France.

1 Make the meringue mixture as directed in the main recipe, substituting 1½ cups ground toasted almonds for the hazelnuts.
2 Shape and bake the meringue rounds as directed.
3 Make the butter cream as directed, substituting Armagnac or Cognac for the kirsch. Alternatively, flavor the butter cream with coffee: dissolve 2 tbsp instant coffee granules in 2 tbsp hot water, cool slightly, and beat into the butter cream.
4 Toast 1 cup sliced almonds in the oven (see box, page 43).
5 Assemble the cake as directed, and decorate with the toasted almonds, instead of hazelnuts, and chocolate-coated coffee beans, if you like.

EXOTIC FRUIT IN TULIP COOKIE CUPS

🍽 SERVES 8   ⏲ WORK TIME 55–65 MINUTES   ☕ BAKING TIME 20–28 MINUTES

EQUIPMENT

- chef's knife
- small knife
- bowls
- large metal spoon
- 7-inch pan lid †
- wooden spoon
- metal spatula
- pencil
- strainer
- pastry brush
- glass jar ‡
- whisk
- 2 baking sheets
- chopping board
- parchment paper

† plate can also be used
‡ small tumbler can also be used

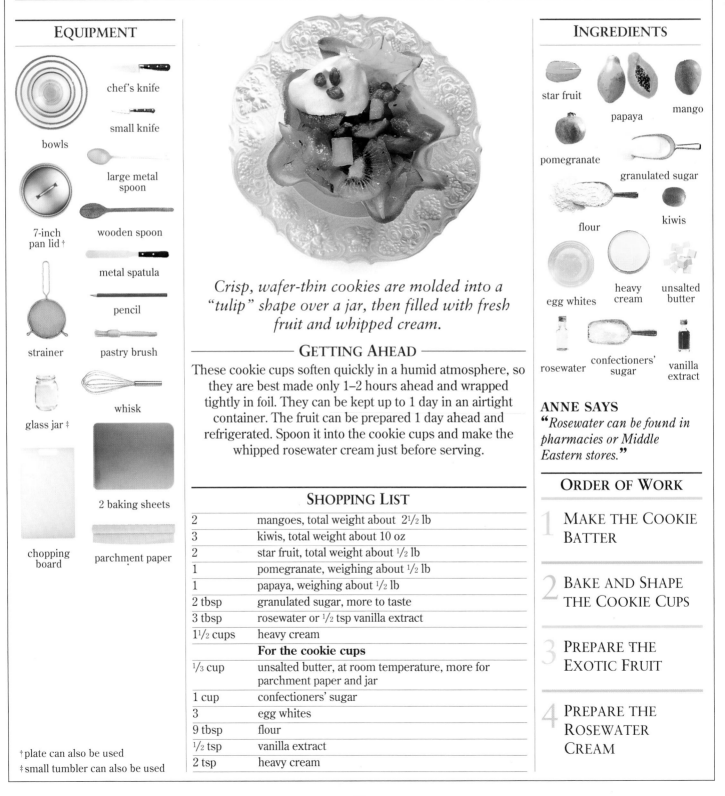

Crisp, wafer-thin cookies are molded into a "tulip" shape over a jar, then filled with fresh fruit and whipped cream.

GETTING AHEAD

These cookie cups soften quickly in a humid atmosphere, so they are best made only 1–2 hours ahead and wrapped tightly in foil. They can be kept up to 1 day in an airtight container. The fruit can be prepared 1 day ahead and refrigerated. Spoon it into the cookie cups and make the whipped rosewater cream just before serving.

SHOPPING LIST

2	mangoes, total weight about 2½ lb
3	kiwis, total weight about 10 oz
2	star fruit, total weight about ½ lb
1	pomegranate, weighing about ½ lb
1	papaya, weighing about ½ lb
2 tbsp	granulated sugar, more to taste
3 tbsp	rosewater or ½ tsp vanilla extract
1½ cups	heavy cream
	For the cookie cups
⅓ cup	unsalted butter, at room temperature, more for parchment paper and jar
1 cup	confectioners' sugar
3	egg whites
9 tbsp	flour
½ tsp	vanilla extract
2 tsp	heavy cream

INGREDIENTS

- star fruit
- papaya
- mango
- pomegranate
- granulated sugar
- flour
- kiwis
- egg whites
- heavy cream
- unsalted butter
- rosewater
- confectioners' sugar
- vanilla extract

ANNE SAYS
"Rosewater can be found in pharmacies or Middle Eastern stores."

ORDER OF WORK

1 MAKE THE COOKIE BATTER

2 BAKE AND SHAPE THE COOKIE CUPS

3 PREPARE THE EXOTIC FRUIT

4 PREPARE THE ROSEWATER CREAM

1 MAKE THE COOKIE BATTER

1 Heat the oven to 400°F. Line each baking sheet with parchment paper. Draw two 7-inch circles on each sheet with a pencil, using the pan lid as a guide. Turn the paper over. Lifting the paper, put a dot of butter in each corner of the baking sheet to help the paper adhere.

2 With the wooden spoon, beat the unsalted butter in a bowl until it becomes pale and creamy. Sift in the confectioners' sugar and beat once again until the mixture is smooth.

3 Gradually add about half of the egg whites to the butter and sugar mixture, beating with the wooden spoon until thoroughly incorporated.

Flour is added alternately with egg whites

4 Sift the flour. Add 1 tbsp of the flour to the batter and mix well, then gently stir in the remaining egg whites a little at a time.

5 Stir in the rest of the flour. Add the vanilla extract and heavy cream, and stir to combine.

ANNE SAYS
"This quantity of batter will make more cookies than you need, to allow for test cookies to be baked."

2 BAKE AND SHAPE THE COOKIE CUPS

Batter should just hold a shape

1 With the back of a spoon, thinly
spread 1½–2 tbsp batter inside
each circle on the baking sheets.
Bake the cookies until brown
around the edges, 5–7 minutes.
Lightly brush the base and side
of the jar with softened butter.

ANNE SAYS
*"It is a good idea to bake a test cookie
at the start. If it is too stiff to shape,
stir 1–2 tbsp melted butter into the
remaining batter. If the cookie is too thin
and fragile, stir in 1–2 tbsp more flour."*

Spread batter
very smoothly so
it bakes evenly

! TAKE CARE !
*These cookies burn easily, so
watch carefully during baking.*

Cookie is hot,
so use metal
spatula for lifting

Mold cookie at once;
it stiffens quickly on
cooling

ANNE SAYS
*"If a cookie becomes too firm to shape,
put it back in the oven for 1 minute to
warm and soften it."*

2 Loosen each of the cookies from
the parchment paper with the
metal spatula. Lift one of them off the
baking sheet and drape it immediately
over the upturned jar.

3 Gently mold the cookie
around the base of the
jar so that it forms a fluted edge.
When cool, remove the cookie from
the jar, and quickly shape the remaining
3 cookies in the same way. Reusing the
parchment paper, continue baking and
shaping the cookies, making 8 in all.

Molded cookie
should form a
deep cup to
hold fruit
filling

3 PREPARE THE EXOTIC FRUIT

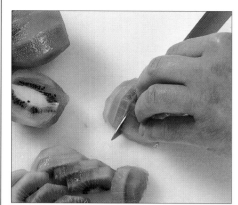

Fresh kiwis are bright green and juicy

Star shape is revealed when fruit is sliced

1 Peel, pit, and cube the mangoes (see box, below). Put the cubes in a large bowl. Trim the ends of the kiwis. Set the kiwis upright and trim off the skin in strips, working from top to bottom. With the chef's knife, cut the fruit lengthwise in half, then cut the halves crosswise into slices. Add the slices to the bowl.

2 Trim and discard the ends from the star fruit. Use the chef's knife to cut the fruit across into 3/8-inch slices, then add them to the bowl.

HOW TO PEEL, PIT, AND CUBE MANGO

Removing the pit from the mango and cubing the flesh by this "hedgehog" method is both simple and neat. It is also less wasteful than other methods.

1 Cut the mango lengthwise on both sides of the pit, so the knife just misses the pit.

2 Cut the remaining mango away from the pit in 2 long slices. Discard the pit.

Mango cubes are easy to remove from skin

3 With a small knife, cut one piece of the mango in a lattice, cutting through the flesh but not the peel.

4 Holding the mango flesh-upward, push the center of the peel with your thumbs to turn it inside out, opening the cuts of flesh to reveal cubes. Cut the cubes away from the skin. Repeat with the other pieces of mango.

4 Working over the bowl, break the pomegranate in half, following the scored lines. Break each half into quarters. Peel the hard skin back from each quarter, releasing the seeds into the bowl. Discard any pieces of membrane. Reserve a few of the seeds for garnish.

3 Using the point of the small knife, trim off the blossom end of the pomegranate. Score the skin into quarters, taking care not to puncture any of the juicy seeds inside.

Try not to crush pomegranate seeds when removing bits of membrane

5 Cut the papaya lengthwise in half. Scoop out and discard the dark seeds, then cut the flesh into quarters.

6 Holding the quarters with the skin side toward you, peel off the skin with the small knife. Cut the papaya flesh into chunks and put them in the bowl.

Small vegetable knife is best for peeling papaya

Make sure all papaya seeds are removed

7 Sprinkle the granulated sugar and rosewater or vanilla over the fruit and stir gently to mix them together. Cover and chill, at least 1 hour.

4 PREPARE THE ROSEWATER CREAM

1 Set the strainer over a bowl. Spoon the fruit into the strainer so the juices drain into the bowl.

Juices from macerating fruit add flavor to whipped cream

2 Pour the cream into a chilled bowl and whip until it forms soft peaks. Add about 3 tbsp of the juices from the fruit and whip until the cream forms soft peaks again and just holds a shape. Taste the cream and add more sugar or rosewater, if necessary.

Rosewater cream is perfect accompaniment to exotic fruit

🍽 TO SERVE

Set a cookie cup on each dessert plate and fill with the fruit. Top each filled cookie with a spoonful of rosewater cream and garnish with the reserved pomegranate seeds. Serve immediately.

Tulip cups should be filled at very last moment so fruit does not soak crisp cookie

VARIATION

WAFER TOWERS WITH EXOTIC FRUIT

The same delicate cookie batter is baked in smaller rounds and stacked with cream and fruit into delectable "towers."

1 Make the cookie batter as directed in the main recipe.
2 Prepare the baking sheets as directed, this time drawing four 4-inch circles on each sheet and using a cookie cutter as a guide. Put about 2–3 tsp batter on each circle and spread evenly to fill it, then bake in the heated oven as directed. Transfer the wafers to a wire rack, keeping them flat, and let cool. Continue baking the wafers to make 24 in all.
3 Prepare the exotic fruit as directed.
4 Whip the cream as directed. Drain the fruit, without reserving the juice. Set aside a few pieces of each fruit for the garnish, then gently fold the whipped cream into the remaining fruit.
5 Set a wafer on each dessert plate. Add a spoonful of the fruit and cream mixture, smoothing the top level. Set a second wafer on top of each.
6 Top with another spoonful of the fruit and cream mixture and crown with a third wafer.
7 Spoon a little of the remaining fruit and cream mixture on top. Garnish the tops and the plates with the reserved fruit, and serve immediately.

RUM-SOAKED RING CAKE

Savarin

🍽 SERVES 8　🥄 WORK TIME 40–50 MINUTES*　🍲 BAKING TIME 30–35 MINUTES

EQUIPMENT

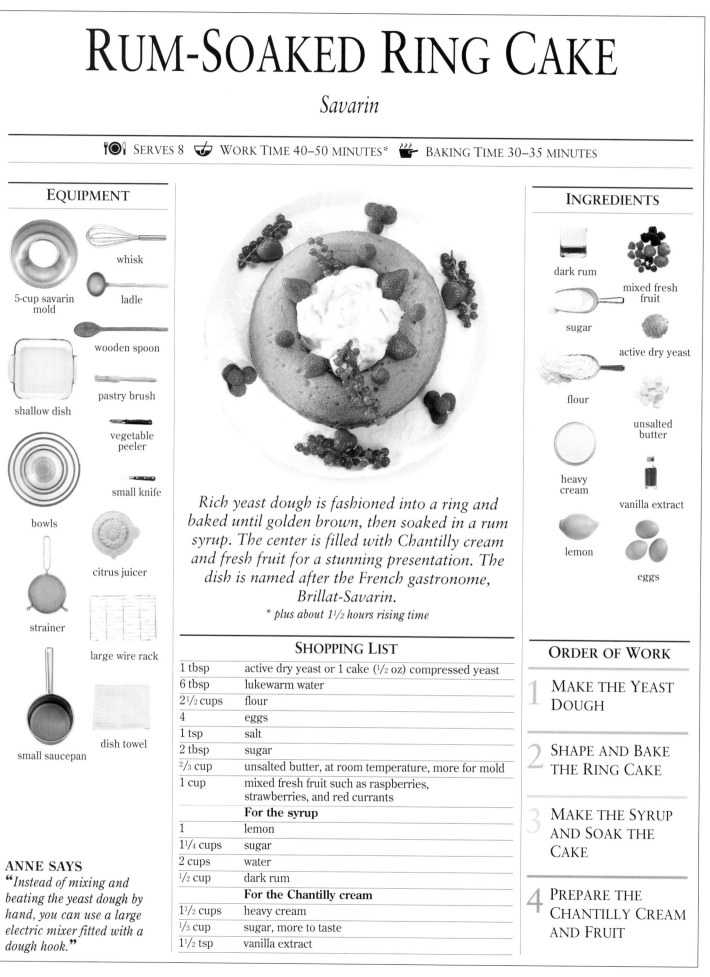

- 5-cup savarin mold
- whisk
- ladle
- wooden spoon
- pastry brush
- shallow dish
- vegetable peeler
- small knife
- bowls
- citrus juicer
- strainer
- large wire rack
- small saucepan
- dish towel

ANNE SAYS
"Instead of mixing and beating the yeast dough by hand, you can use a large electric mixer fitted with a dough hook."

Rich yeast dough is fashioned into a ring and baked until golden brown, then soaked in a rum syrup. The center is filled with Chantilly cream and fresh fruit for a stunning presentation. The dish is named after the French gastronome, Brillat-Savarin.

* plus about 1½ hours rising time

INGREDIENTS

- dark rum
- mixed fresh fruit
- sugar
- active dry yeast
- flour
- unsalted butter
- heavy cream
- vanilla extract
- lemon
- eggs

SHOPPING LIST

1 tbsp	active dry yeast or 1 cake (½ oz) compressed yeast
6 tbsp	lukewarm water
2½ cups	flour
4	eggs
1 tsp	salt
2 tbsp	sugar
²/₃ cup	unsalted butter, at room temperature, more for mold
1 cup	mixed fresh fruit such as raspberries, strawberries, and red currants
	For the syrup
1	lemon
1¼ cups	sugar
2 cups	water
½ cup	dark rum
	For the Chantilly cream
1½ cups	heavy cream
⅓ cup	sugar, more to taste
1½ tsp	vanilla extract

ORDER OF WORK

1. **MAKE THE YEAST DOUGH**

2. **SHAPE AND BAKE THE RING CAKE**

3. **MAKE THE SYRUP AND SOAK THE CAKE**

4. **PREPARE THE CHANTILLY CREAM AND FRUIT**

1 MAKE THE YEAST DOUGH

1 Sprinkle or crumble the yeast over the warm water in a small bowl and leave until dissolved, about 5 minutes.

2 Sift the flour into a large bowl and make a well in the center. Add the eggs, salt, sugar, and yeast mixture to the well in the flour.

Yeast should be completely dissolved before adding to eggs

Your hand is best tool for mixing yeast batter because warmth helps mixture to rise

3 Mix the ingredients together in the well with one hand, holding the bowl with the other. Gradually draw in the flour from the side and mix to form a smooth dough.

4 Tilt the bowl slightly and beat the dough: cup your hand like a spoon and, with your palm upward, lift the dough, then let it fall back into the bowl with a slap. Continue beating the dough in this way until it is very elastic, about 5 minutes.

Pinch and squeeze butter with your hand to work it into dough

5 Cover the bowl with the dampened dish towel. Let stand in a warm place until the dough has doubled in bulk, 45–60 minutes.

6 Knead the dough lightly with your hand to knock out the air. In a small bowl, cream the butter to soften it, then beat it into the dough.

2 SHAPE AND BAKE THE RING CAKE

1 Heat the oven to 400°F. Brush the mold with melted butter. Freeze the mold until the butter is hard, about 10 minutes, then butter the mold again.

ANNE SAYS

"This double coating gives the cake a golden surface and helps prevent it from sticking to the mold."

2 Spoon the dough into the mold, letting it fall evenly around the bottom; it should fill the mold by about one-third.

3 Cover the mold with an upturned clean bowl and leave in a warm place until the dough has risen to the top of the mold, about 35–40 minutes.

Bowl covers mold securely, keeping dough warm

Risen dough should just reach top of mold

4 Bake the cake in the heated oven until brown and pulling away from the side of the mold, 30–35 minutes. Let cool, 5 minutes. Run the small knife around the edge of the cake and turn it out onto the wire rack set over the shallow dish. Let cool to lukewarm.

3 MAKE THE SYRUP AND SOAK THE CAKE

1 With the vegetable peeler, pare the zest from the lemon. Cut the lemon in half, squeeze the juice, and reserve. Heat the sugar with the water in the saucepan until dissolved. Bring to a boil, then add the lemon zest, and simmer 5 minutes.

2 Remove the saucepan from the heat. Stir the lemon juice and half of the rum into the syrup.

3 Ladle the syrup over the cake. Reheat any syrup that runs off into the dish and ladle it back over the cake. Continue ladling the syrup over the cake in this way until it has all been absorbed. The cake will swell and become glossy. Let cool completely.

4 PREPARE THE CHANTILLY CREAM AND FRUIT

1 Pour the cream into a chilled bowl and whip until soft peaks form. Add the sugar and vanilla extract and whip until soft peaks form again. Refrigerate the Chantilly cream until ready to serve. Pick over the fruit, washing it only if it is dirty.

2 Transfer the cake to a serving plate and sprinkle with the remaining rum. Spoon the Chantilly cream into the center of the ring cake.

ANNE SAYS
"Be sure cake is cool before adding whipped cream."

Ring cake is perfect container for Chantilly cream

🍽 **TO SERVE**
Decorate the ring cake and the platter around it with the mixed fresh fruit.

Fresh fruit – whatever is in season – makes a beautiful finish for cake

Rum-soaked cake can be made well ahead

RUM BABAS

In the 18th century, Duke Stanislas of Lorraine is said to have named these little cakes after Ali Baba, his favorite character in A Thousand and One Nights.

1 Omit the fruit. Make the yeast dough and let rise, as directed.
2 Work in 1/2 cup currants with the butter, distributing them evenly.
3 Thoroughly butter 8 bucket-shaped baba or dariole molds or small ring-shaped baba molds, each 3/4-cup capacity. Divide the dough among the molds, filling them one-third full. Cover and let rise, 25 minutes.
4 Bake in the heated oven until the cakes begin to shrink from the sides of the molds, 15–20 minutes. Unmold the cakes and let them cool.
5 Make the syrup, omitting the lemon.
6 Put the cakes into the pan of syrup and spoon it over them until it is all absorbed. Let cool completely.
7 Just before serving, sprinkle each cake with 2 tsp rum. Serve the babas lying on their sides, sliced, if you like. Accompany with Chantilly cream.

GETTING AHEAD
The cake can be baked 1 week ahead; store in an airtight container. The drier it is, the more syrup it will absorb. Soak no more than 2 hours ahead; add fruit and cream before serving.

CHESTNUT NAPOLEONS

🍽 SERVES 6–8　🥣 WORK TIME 2 HOURS*　♨ BAKING TIME 20–25 MINUTES

EQUIPMENT

rolling pin

pastry scraper

metal spatula

chef's knife

whisk

bowls

large wide spatula

rubber spatula

strainer

ruler

medium saucepan

large baking sheet

large rectangular wire rack

cardboard　parchment paper

metal skewer

serrated knife

scissors

ANNE SAYS
"*Puff pastry dough must be kept cold when rolled, so a marble slab is ideal. Or, place a roasting pan filled with ice water on the work surface for 15 minutes. Dry the surface before rolling the dough.*"

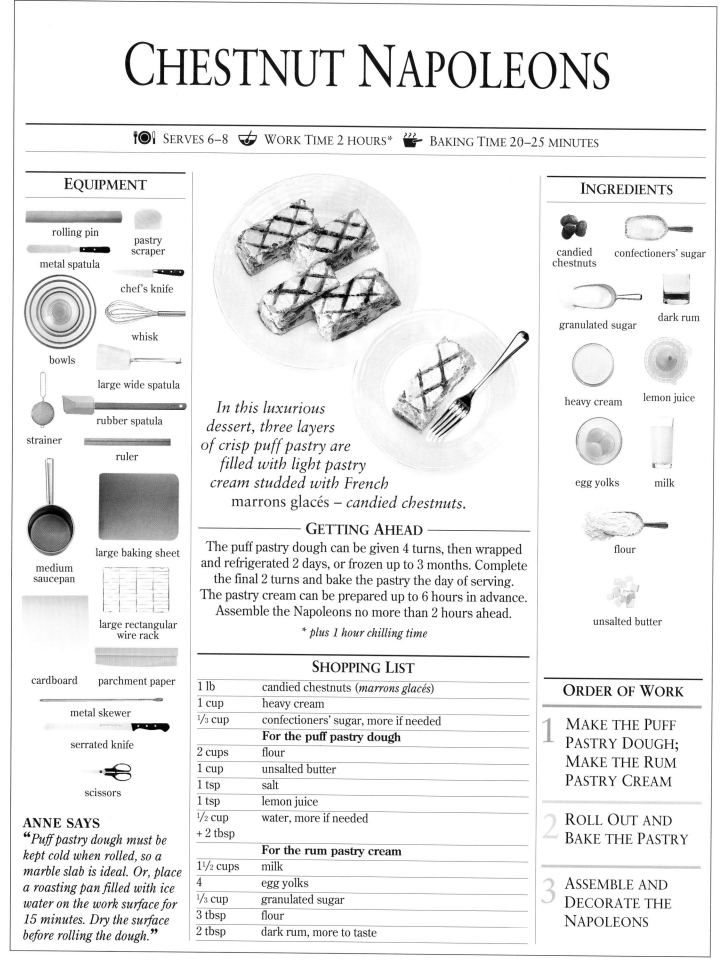

In this luxurious dessert, three layers of crisp puff pastry are filled with light pastry cream studded with French marrons glacés – *candied chestnuts.*

GETTING AHEAD

The puff pastry dough can be given 4 turns, then wrapped and refrigerated 2 days, or frozen up to 3 months. Complete the final 2 turns and bake the pastry the day of serving. The pastry cream can be prepared up to 6 hours in advance. Assemble the Napoleons no more than 2 hours ahead.

* plus 1 hour chilling time

SHOPPING LIST

1 lb	candied chestnuts (*marrons glacés*)
1 cup	heavy cream
1/3 cup	confectioners' sugar, more if needed
	For the puff pastry dough
2 cups	flour
1 cup	unsalted butter
1 tsp	salt
1 tsp	lemon juice
1/2 cup + 2 tbsp	water, more if needed
	For the rum pastry cream
1 1/2 cups	milk
4	egg yolks
1/3 cup	granulated sugar
3 tbsp	flour
2 tbsp	dark rum, more to taste

INGREDIENTS

candied chestnuts

confectioners' sugar

granulated sugar

dark rum

heavy cream

lemon juice

egg yolks

milk

flour

unsalted butter

ORDER OF WORK

1　**MAKE THE PUFF PASTRY DOUGH; MAKE THE RUM PASTRY CREAM**

2　**ROLL OUT AND BAKE THE PASTRY**

3　**ASSEMBLE AND DECORATE THE NAPOLEONS**

1 MAKE THE PUFF PASTRY DOUGH; MAKE THE RUM PASTRY CREAM

1 Make the puff pastry dough (see pages 60–61), and chill, wrapped, in the refrigerator.

2 Scald the milk in the saucepan, bringing it just to a boil. Meanwhile, whisk the egg yolks with the granulated sugar until thick and pale, 2–3 minutes. Whisk in the flour.

Flour and egg yolks both thicken pastry cream

3 Gradually stir the hot milk into the egg yolks and sugar until the mixture is smooth.

Stir with whisk when adding milk

Mixture should be free from lumps

4 Pour the pastry cream back into the saucepan and return the saucepan to medium heat.

5 Bring the pastry cream to a boil, whisking constantly until it thickens. Reduce the heat to low and cook, still whisking, until slightly softened, about 2 minutes.

! TAKE CARE !
If lumps form, remove from the heat at once and whisk until the cream is smooth again.

6 Remove from the heat. Let the cream cool, then stir in the rum, adding more to taste. Transfer the cream to a bowl, cover, and chill, at least 1 hour. Meanwhile, roll out and bake the pastry sheet.

Pastry cream must be cool before adding rum, or alcohol will evaporate

HOW TO MAKE PUFF PASTRY DOUGH

Puff pastry dough is the lightest, and yet the richest, of all the pastry doughs, composed of literally hundreds of layers of flour-and-water dough interleaved with unsalted butter.

1 Sift the flour onto the work surface and make a well in the center. Cut 2 tbsp of the butter into pieces and add to the well with the salt, lemon juice, and water.

2 Quickly blend the butter, salt, lemon juice, and water together in the well with your fingertips.

3 Gradually draw in the flour, working with your fingertips, to form coarse crumbs. If the crumbs seem dry, add a little more water to form a dough.

4 With the pastry scraper, cut and turn the dough several times until it forms a rough, slightly moist ball.

ANNE SAYS
"At this stage, try to handle the dough as little as possible."

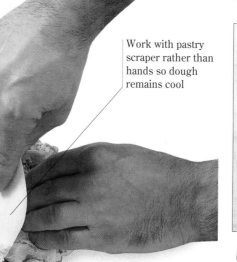

Work with pastry scraper rather than hands so dough remains cool

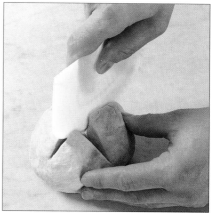

5 Score the dough with the pastry scraper to prevent shrinkage, then wrap and chill, 15 minutes.

6 Lightly flour the remaining butter. Pound the butter with the rolling pin, folding and pounding it until it is softened and pliable.

7 With the pastry scraper, shape the piece of butter into a 5-inch square.

ANNE SAYS
"The butter should be pounded until it is the same consistency as the dough, making it easy to roll them together."

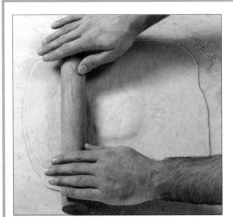

Wrap dough closely around butter

8 Roll out the chilled dough on the lightly floured surface to a 10-inch square that is slightly thicker in the center than at the sides.

9 Set the square of butter diagonally in the center and pull the corners of the dough around the butter to wrap it like an envelope. Pinch the edges together with your fingers to seal them.

10 Lightly flour the work surface again and turn the dough package over onto it, seam-side down. Tap the dough several times with the rolling pin to flatten it.

Roll dough with firm, even pressure

11 Roll out the dough to a rectangle about 6 inches wide and 18 inches long, keeping the corners square and the thickness even.

ANNE SAYS
"Work briskly and roll the dough away from you, keeping it moving on the floured surface."

12 Neatly fold the rectangle of dough in three, like a business letter, so that it forms a square.

ANNE SAYS
"Each rolling out and folding of the pastry dough is called a turn."

13 Turn the dough square 90° to bring the seam-side to your right. Gently press the layered ends with the rolling pin to seal them. This completes the first turn. Repeat steps 11, 12, and 13 to complete a second turn.

Before pressing and rolling, turn dough so 1 layered end faces you

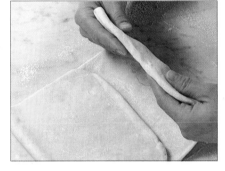

14 Mark the number of turns in one corner of the dough with your fingertips. Wrap the dough and chill, 15 minutes. Repeat these double rollings twice more to make a total of 6 turns, chilling 15 minutes after each set of 2 turns.

2 ROLL OUT AND BAKE THE PASTRY

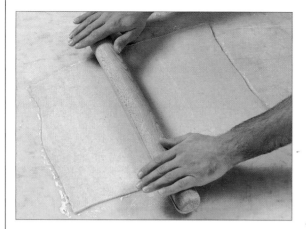

Use rolling pin to transfer dough to baking sheet

1 Heat the oven to 400°F. Sprinkle the baking sheet with cold water. Roll out the chilled puff pastry dough to a thin rectangular sheet, about ⅛ inch thick. The sheet of dough should be slightly larger than the baking sheet.

2 Roll the dough around the rolling pin, then unroll it onto the baking sheet, letting the edges overhang slightly. Chill the dough, 15 minutes.

ANNE SAYS
"Press the dough down lightly on the baking sheet, making sure the edges overhang, so it does not shrink in the oven."

Parchment paper prevents rack marking dough deeply

3 Prick the dough all over with a fork. Place a sheet of parchment paper on the dough, then set the wire rack on top. Bake the dough in the heated oven until it begins to brown, 15–20 minutes.

ANNE SAYS
"Pricking the dough and setting the parchment paper and wire rack on top ensure that it cooks thoroughly in an even layer without rising too high."

4 Turn over the dough: holding the wire rack and baking sheet together, turn them over so the pastry falls onto the rack. Slide the baking sheet under the pastry. Continue baking the pastry until both sides are well browned, about 10 minutes longer.

ANNE SAYS
"*The pastry should be thoroughly browned for the best flavor; however, if it is browning too quickly, cover loosely with foil.*"

Turning ensures pastry is thoroughly cooked underneath

When cool, pastry trimmings are easy to crush

Pastry stays crisp when cooled on rack

5 Remove the baking sheet from the oven and carefully slide the pastry onto a chopping board. While the pastry is still warm, trim the edges with the chef's knife to neaten them. Cut the rectangle of pastry lengthwise into 3 equal strips.

6 Transfer the pastry strips to the wire rack and let cool completely. With the rolling pin, crush the pastry trimmings to make fine crumbs, and reserve.

3 ASSEMBLE AND DECORATE THE NAPOLEONS

Leave some large pieces of candied chestnut for texture

1 With your fingertips, coarsely crumble the candied chestnuts into a small bowl. Pour the cream into a chilled bowl and whip until soft peaks form.

2 Fold the whipped cream into the chilled rum pastry cream: cut down into the center of the bowl with the rubber spatula, scoop under the contents, and turn them over in a rolling motion. At the same time, with your other hand, turn the bowl counter-clockwise. Continue until combined.

4 Sprinkle half of the crumbled candied chestnuts evenly over the pastry cream filling.

3 Cut a sheet of cardboard to the same size as the pastry strips. Set one strip of pastry on top. With the metal spatula, spread half of the pastry cream filling over the pastry strip to cover it evenly.

Sprinkle chestnuts into corners as well as center of filling

5 Put another strip of pastry on top and cover with the remaining pastry cream filling and candied chestnuts.

Tap strainer against your hand so sugar falls evenly

6 Add the last pastry strip and press down lightly. Sift the confectioners' sugar thickly over the top of the assembled pastry.

7 Smooth out any cream filling on the sides. Press the reserved pastry crumbs onto the sides to coat thinly.

8 Heat the metal skewer: hold it over a burner until it is red hot, using a folded dish towel to protect your hand. Toast a criss-cross pattern in the sugar, reheating the skewer as necessary.

TO SERVE

Cut into slices: hold the wide spatula vertically to support the end and, with the serrated knife, cut crosswise in a sawing motion, taking care not to squash the cream filling.

ANNE SAYS
"An electric knife makes slicing easier."

VARIATION

CHOCOLATE NAPOLEONS

Chocolate replaces the candied chestnuts in this variation, and the slices are coated with pastry crumbs on all sides then piped with decorative trails of melted white chocolate.

1 Omit the candied chestnuts and rum. Make the puff pastry dough and bake the pastry.

2 Cut 8 oz semisweet chocolate into large chunks. Chop them with the chef's knife, or in a food processor using the pulse button. Heat the chocolate in a bowl set in a saucepan half-filled with hot water. Stir chocolate occasionally until melted and smooth. Let the chocolate cool.

3 Make the pastry cream as directed, adding brandy instead of rum. When cool, stir in two-thirds of the cooled melted chocolate. Pour 1 1/2 cups heavy cream into a chilled bowl and whip until stiff peaks form. Fold the cream into the chocolate pastry cream, using a rubber spatula.

4 With a metal spatula, evenly spread the remaining melted chocolate over one of the pastry strips to cover it completely. Let it set.

5 Place another of the remaining pastry strips on a sheet of cardboard, as directed, and spread with half of the chocolate pastry cream. Put the remaining strip of pastry on top, and spread with the rest of the chocolate pastry cream. Finally, cover with the chocolate-coated pastry strip.

6 With the serrated knife, cut the dessert into 6–8 slices. Press reserved pastry crumbs on the sides of each slice, as directed.

7 Chop and melt 1 oz white chocolate. Let cool slightly, then put it into one corner of a small plastic bag. Twist the bag to enclose the chocolate and snip off the tip of the corner. Pipe decorative trails of chocolate on top of each dark-chocolate-coated Napoleon.

Stripes of caramelized sugar are an easy and attractive decoration

COCONUT AND PINEAPPLE MOUSSE CAKE

🍽 SERVES 8 🥄 WORK TIME 1¼ HOURS* ♨ BAKING TIME 30–40 MINUTES

EQUIPMENT

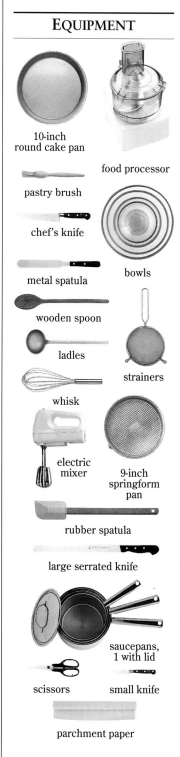

10-inch round cake pan

food processor

pastry brush

chef's knife

metal spatula

bowls

wooden spoon

ladles

strainers

whisk

electric mixer

9-inch springform pan

rubber spatula

large serrated knife

saucepans, 1 with lid

scissors

small knife

parchment paper

In this light and fragrant cake, a creamy pineapple mousse is layered with coconut sponge cake rounds and decorated with toasted coconut.
* plus at least 2 hours chilling time

SHOPPING LIST

For the coconut cake	
¼ cup	unsalted butter, more for cake pan
4	eggs
1 tsp	vanilla extract
⅔ cup	granulated sugar
1 cup	flour, more for cake pan
	salt
6 tbsp	unsweetened shredded coconut
For the pineapple mousse filling	
1	pineapple, weighing 2½–3 lb
	juice of 1 lime
⅔ cup	light brown sugar
2 tbsp	powdered gelatin
2 cups	heavy cream
2	eggs
2	egg yolks
¼ cup	granulated sugar
For the decoration	
6 tbsp	unsweetened shredded coconut
⅔ cup	apricot jam
	candied lime slices (see box, page 71), optional

INGREDIENTS

unsweetened shredded coconut

egg yolks

pineapple

eggs

vanilla extract

unsalted butter

flour

granulated sugar

apricot jam

lime juice

powdered gelatin

heavy cream

light brown sugar

ORDER OF WORK

1 MAKE THE COCONUT CAKE ROUNDS

2 PREPARE THE PINEAPPLE

3 LINE THE SPRINGFORM PAN

4 MAKE THE MOUSSE FILLING

5 ASSEMBLE AND DECORATE THE CAKE

1 MAKE THE COCONUT CAKE ROUNDS

1 Heat the oven to 350°F. Butter the cake pan and line the bottom with parchment paper. Butter the paper. Sprinkle in 2–3 tbsp flour and turn the pan to coat it; tap the pan upside down to remove excess. Melt the butter in a pan; let cool until tepid. Sift the flour with a pinch of salt into a medium bowl.

2 In a large bowl, beat the eggs with the electric mixer for a few seconds to mix. Add the vanilla extract and sugar and continue beating at high speed until the mixture is pale and thick, and leaves a ribbon trail when the beaters are lifted, about 5 minutes.

3 Sift one-third of the flour mixture over the egg mixture; cut and fold them together. Add another third of the flour and fold together in the same way.

Rubber spatula is excellent tool for folding

Sifted flour falls lightly onto airy egg mixture

4 Add the remaining flour with the cooled melted butter and the shredded coconut. Fold them in gently but thoroughly.

6 Cool the cake slightly, then turn out onto a wire rack, peel off the parchment paper, and let cool completely. Meanwhile, prepare the pineapple.

Peel off paper as soon as cake is unmolded so steam can escape

5 Pour the batter into the prepared cake pan, then tap the pan on a work surface to level the batter and knock out any air bubbles. Bake the cake in the heated oven until risen and just firm to the touch, 30–40 minutes.

2 PREPARE THE PINEAPPLE

1 Cut off the plume and base of the pineapple, then peel it: work from top to bottom following the curve of the fruit and cutting deeply enough to remove the eyes with the skin.

ANNE SAYS
"You can use two 16-oz cans of pineapple chunks in syrup instead of the poached pineapple used here. In this case, use the syrup from the can in place of the poaching syrup in step 4."

2 Cut the pineapple lengthwise in half and then into quarters. Cut out the core from each quarter. Cut the quarters crosswise into neat chunks.

3 Heat the lime juice with the brown sugar and 1/2 cup water in a medium saucepan, stirring occasionally, until the sugar has dissolved. Bring to a boil and boil 1 minute. Add the pineapple chunks to the pan. Cover the pan and poach until the pineapple is just tender when pierced with the tip of the small knife, 8–10 minutes.

Tip pineapple into strainer

4 Set a strainer over a bowl and drain the pineapple. Reserve 1/2 cup of the poaching syrup.

5 Reserve 8–10 pineapple chunks for decoration. Transfer the remaining pineapple chunks to the food processor or a blender, and work to a purée. There should be about 1 1/2 cups.

ANNE SAYS
"If there is not enough purée, stir in a little poaching syrup."

3 LINE THE SPRINGFORM PAN

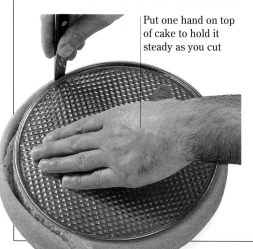

Put one hand on top of cake to hold it steady as you cut

1 When the cake is cold, trim the edge with the small knife to fit inside the springform pan, using the base of the pan as a guide. Cut the cake horizontally in half with the serrated knife, using a sawing action.

2 Cut a 9-inch round of cardboard and fit it in the bottom of the springform pan. Lightly oil the side of the pan. Put 1 cake round on the bottom, cut-side up. Set aside.

4 MAKE THE MOUSSE FILLING

Be sure gelatin is sprinkled evenly

1 Pour the reserved pineapple syrup into a small saucepan and sprinkle the gelatin evenly on the surface. Let soak, about 5 minutes. The gelatin will soften to a spongy consistency.

2 Pour the cream into a chilled bowl. Whip with a whisk or an electric mixer just until it forms soft peaks. Cover and chill the cream while preparing the rest of the filling.

3 Combine the eggs, egg yolks, granulated sugar, and pineapple purée in a medium saucepan, and whisk until well blended. Cook the mixture, stirring, just until it boils.

Pour melted gelatin in a thin, steady stream

5 Set the saucepan of gelatin over very low heat and melt it until it is pourable, shaking the saucepan occasionally, 1–2 minutes. Do not stir it, or it may form lumps. Whisk the gelatin mixture into the tepid pineapple mixture. Continue whisking until cool.

Whisk constantly so gelatin is incorporated evenly

4 Pour the pineapple mixture into a large bowl and whisk with the electric mixer or hand whisk until it is pale and has cooled to tepid, 5–7 minutes.

Pineapple mixture will thicken as it cools

6 Set the bowl in a larger bowl of ice water and stir with the rubber spatula until the pineapple mixture begins to thicken.

7 Working quickly, fold in the whipped cream with the rubber spatula: cut down into the center of the bowl, scoop under the contents, and turn the mixture over with a rolling motion.

5 ASSEMBLE AND DECORATE THE CAKE

1 Ladle about half of the pineapple mousse filling onto the cake round in the springform pan and shake gently to level the surface. Set the second cake round, cut-side down, on top of the mousse and press down lightly.

Cake round is cut to fit tightly in pan

2 Ladle the remaining pineapple mousse filling into the cake pan and shake the pan gently again to level the surface. Cover and chill until the filling is firmly set, at least 2 hours.

3 Meanwhile, heat the oven to 375°F. For the decoration: spread the shredded coconut in the cake pan and toast in the oven, stirring occasionally, about 5 minutes. Let cool.

4 Make the apricot jam glaze: melt the jam with 2–3 tbsp water in a small saucepan, stirring occasionally. Work through a strainer. Return to the saucepan and melt again.

5 Take the pineapple mousse cake from the refrigerator, carefully loosen the side of the springform pan, and remove it.

Sprinkle coconut carefully, close to band of diced pineapple

6 Set the cake, still on the base of the pan, on a large bowl to raise it off the work surface. With the pastry brush, coat the side of the cake with the warm apricot jam glaze.

7 Gently press some toasted coconut onto the side of the cake. Dice the reserved pineapple chunks and arrange in a band on the top of the cake. Sprinkle coconut on both sides of the band of pineapple. Arrange candied lime slices on top, if you like.

How to Make Candied Lime Slices

Candied lime slices make an attractive decoration. Orange slices can be used instead, but they do not need to be simmered in water.

1 Cut 1 lime crosswise into ¹/₈-inch slices; discard the ends. Lay the lime slices in a frying pan, cover with cold water, and bring to a boil. Simmer the slices until the rind has softened but the flesh is still intact, 7–10 minutes. Drain the lime slices, and cut in half, if you like.

2 Sprinkle 1 tbsp sugar over the bottom of the pan. Arrange the lime slices on top, and sprinkle with another 1 tbsp sugar. Cook over low heat until the sugar has caramelized slightly and the fruit is translucent, about 10 minutes. Drain the slices and cool on a wire rack.

¶◎¶ TO SERVE

Carefully transfer the mousse cake on the cardboard round to a flat serving plate.

Candied lime slices are an optional decoration

Pineapple gives Caribbean flavor to creamy dessert

VARIATION
CITRUS MOUSSE CAKE
Orange and lemon replace pineapple, adding bright flavor to this mousse cake.

1 Omit the pineapple, shredded coconut, and apricot jam glaze. Make the sponge cake batter, omitting the coconut. Bake the cake and shape the rounds as directed.
2 Finely grate the zest from 1 lemon. Squeeze the juice from 1¹/₂ lemons; there should be ¹/₄ cup juice. Squeeze the juice from 2 oranges; there should be ³/₄ cup juice.
3 Dissolve the gelatin in ¹/₂ cup of the orange juice in a small saucepan.
4 Make the mousse filling as directed, substituting the lemon juice and remaining orange juice for the pineapple purée, adding the lemon zest, and increasing the sugar to 7 tbsp.
5 Assemble the cake and citrus mousse as directed.
6 Make a candied orange slice decoration, if you like: cut 1 small orange crosswise into ¹/₈-inch slices; discard the ends. Candy the orange slices (see box left, step 2), adding 2 tbsp water when adding the second amount of sugar.
7 Decorate the top of the citrus mousse cake with twisted candied orange slices, if you like.

—— GETTING AHEAD ——
The mousse cake can be made 1 day ahead; keep it, tightly covered in its pan, in the refrigerator. Unmold the cake and add the decoration not more than 2 hours before serving.

CHOCOLATE NUT FONDUE

🍴 SERVES 6   🥣 WORK TIME 25–30 MINUTES   🍲 COOKING TIME 3–5 MINUTES

EQUIPMENT

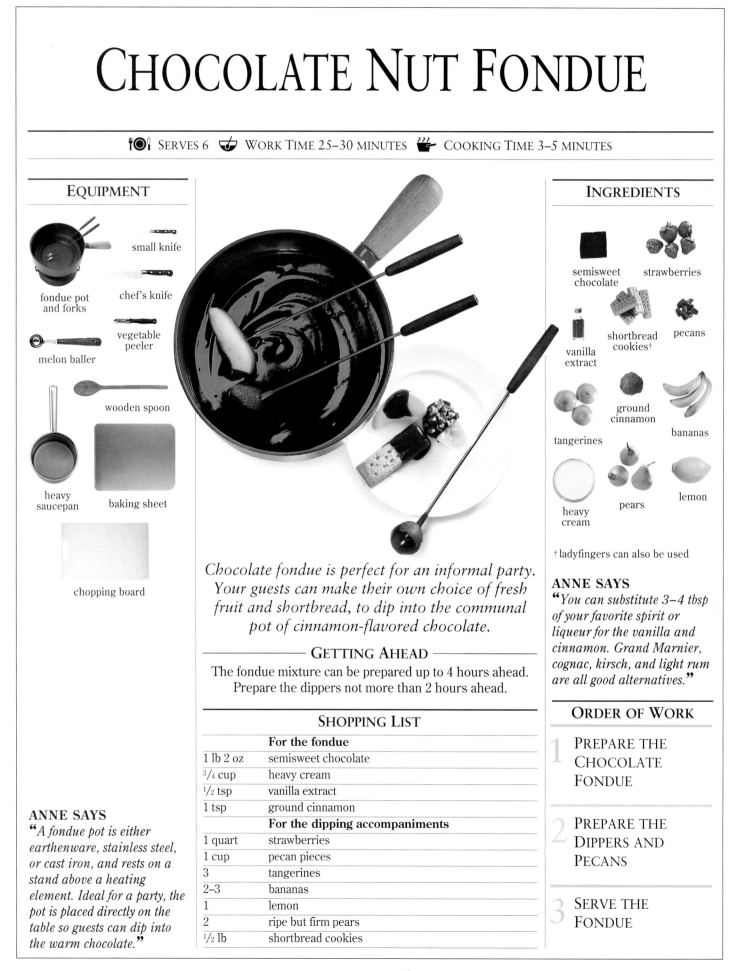

small knife

fondue pot and forks

chef's knife

melon baller

vegetable peeler

wooden spoon

heavy saucepan

baking sheet

chopping board

ANNE SAYS
"A fondue pot is either earthenware, stainless steel, or cast iron, and rests on a stand above a heating element. Ideal for a party, the pot is placed directly on the table so guests can dip into the warm chocolate."

INGREDIENTS

semisweet chocolate

strawberries

vanilla extract

shortbread cookies†

pecans

tangerines

ground cinnamon

bananas

heavy cream

pears

lemon

† ladyfingers can also be used

ANNE SAYS
"You can substitute 3–4 tbsp of your favorite spirit or liqueur for the vanilla and cinnamon. Grand Marnier, cognac, kirsch, and light rum are all good alternatives."

ORDER OF WORK

1   PREPARE THE CHOCOLATE FONDUE

2   PREPARE THE DIPPERS AND PECANS

3   SERVE THE FONDUE

Chocolate fondue is perfect for an informal party. Your guests can make their own choice of fresh fruit and shortbread, to dip into the communal pot of cinnamon-flavored chocolate.

GETTING AHEAD

The fondue mixture can be prepared up to 4 hours ahead. Prepare the dippers not more than 2 hours ahead.

SHOPPING LIST

	For the fondue
1 lb 2 oz	semisweet chocolate
³/₄ cup	heavy cream
¹/₂ tsp	vanilla extract
1 tsp	ground cinnamon
	For the dipping accompaniments
1 quart	strawberries
1 cup	pecan pieces
3	tangerines
2–3	bananas
1	lemon
2	ripe but firm pears
¹/₂ lb	shortbread cookies

1 PREPARE THE CHOCOLATE FONDUE

1 Cut the chocolate into large chunks. Chop them with the chef's knife, or in a food processor using the pulse button. Transfer the chocolate to the saucepan and pour in the cream.

2 Heat gently, stirring until the chocolate has melted and is the consistency of heavy cream. If necessary, simmer a few minutes to the right consistency, stirring constantly. Remove from the heat and stir in the vanilla and cinnamon.

Chop chocolate into even pieces so it melts quickly

Melt chocolate gently so it does not scorch

2 PREPARE THE DIPPERS AND PECANS

1 Heat the oven to 375°F. Hull the strawberries and wash them only if they are dirty. If they are very large, cut them in half.

2 Put the pecans on the baking sheet and spread them out. Toast them in the heated oven until golden, about 5 minutes, stirring them occasionally so that they brown evenly. Remove from the oven and let cool.

3 Peel the tangerines and divide them into sections, discarding any seeds.

Remove chewy pith and membrane from sections

Strawberries for dipping should be ripe but firm

4 Peel the bananas and cut them crosswise on the diagonal into slices ¹/₂ inch thick. Cut the lemon in half, and sprinkle the juice over the banana slices to keep them from turning brown.

5 Peel the pears with the vegetable peeler and cut them lengthwise in half. Remove the cores with the melon baller or with a teaspoon. Cut out the stem end with the small knife.

Hold pear half in one hand while scraping out core

Melon baller removes core neatly

6 Cut each pear half lengthwise into wedges. Sprinkle the pear wedges with lemon juice to keep them from turning brown.

7 Arrange the prepared fruit and shortbread cookies in rows on a large platter.

Arrange dippers so colors contrast

8 With the chef's knife, chop the toasted pecans and put them in a small serving bowl.

3 SERVE THE FONDUE

1 Gently reheat the chocolate mixture, if necessary, and pour it into the fondue pot. Set the pot on the fondue stand at the table. Light the flame and set it to low.

! TAKE CARE !
Chocolate scorches easily, so do not overheat the fondue.

Lower dippers briefly into chocolate for light coating

2 Pass the platter of dippers so guests can dip their own choice of fruit or shortbread into the chocolate fondue and then into the chopped nuts, using their fondue fork.

Fondue forks with long handles are best for dipping

ANNE SAYS
"Tart fruit and crunchy nuts are perfect foil for rich chocolate."

CHOCOLATE COCONUT FONDUE

Orange flavors the chocolate sauce for this fondue, which is served with toasted coconut, giving a tropical accent.

1 Omit the cream, pears, shortbread cookies, and pecans. Prepare the chocolate fondue as directed, omitting the ground cinnamon and using the strained juice of 2 oranges instead of the heavy cream.
2 Prepare the strawberries and bananas as directed.
3 Spread out $1^1/_3$ cups shredded coconut on a baking tray and toast as directed for the pecans.
4 Peel a $2^1/_2$-lb pineapple: cut off the plume and base and set the pineapple upright, base down, on a chopping board. Cut away the peel in strips, working from top to bottom, following the curve of the fruit and cutting deeply enough to remove the eyes with the skin. Cut the pineapple lengthwise in half, then into quarters. Cut out the core from each quarter. Cut the quarters lengthwise into 3–4 strips, then crosswise into neat chunks.
5 Cut an 8-oz pound cake or angel food cake into 1-inch cubes.
6 Arrange the prepared fruit and the cake on a large platter.
7 Serve the fondue as directed, with the prepared fruit and cake for dipping and the toasted coconut for coating.

BAKED ALASKA

EQUIPMENT

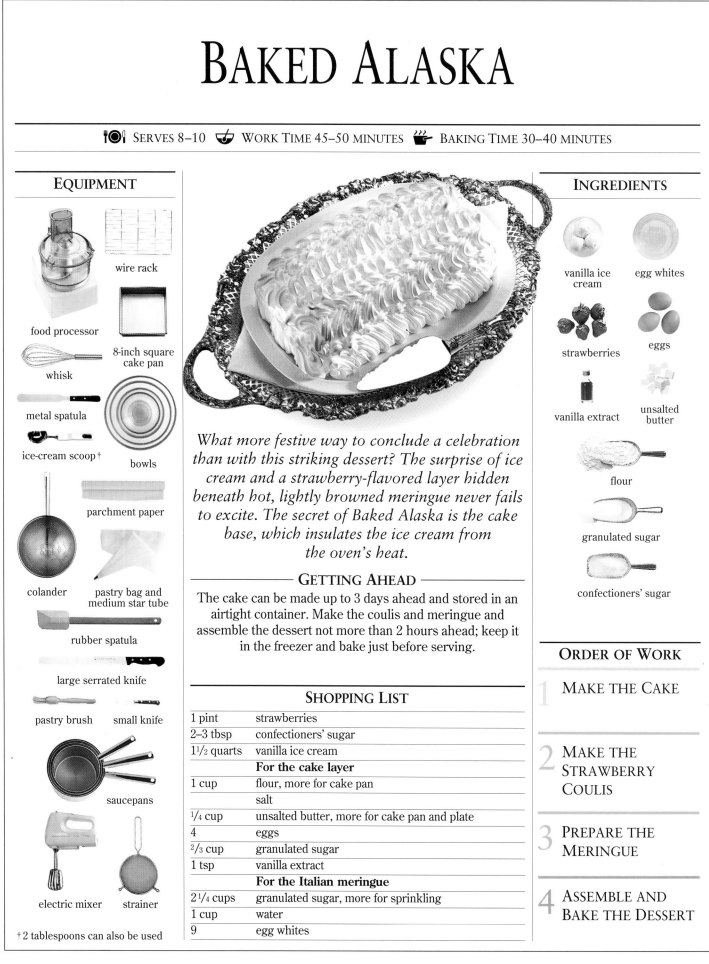

food processor

wire rack

8-inch square cake pan

whisk

metal spatula

ice-cream scoop †

bowls

colander

parchment paper

pastry bag and medium star tube

rubber spatula

large serrated knife

pastry brush   small knife

saucepans

electric mixer   strainer

† 2 tablespoons can also be used

INGREDIENTS

vanilla ice cream

egg whites

strawberries

eggs

vanilla extract

unsalted butter

flour

granulated sugar

confectioners' sugar

What more festive way to conclude a celebration than with this striking dessert? The surprise of ice cream and a strawberry-flavored layer hidden beneath hot, lightly browned meringue never fails to excite. The secret of Baked Alaska is the cake base, which insulates the ice cream from the oven's heat.

GETTING AHEAD

The cake can be made up to 3 days ahead and stored in an airtight container. Make the coulis and meringue and assemble the dessert not more than 2 hours ahead; keep it in the freezer and bake just before serving.

SHOPPING LIST

1 pint	strawberries
2–3 tbsp	confectioners' sugar
1½ quarts	vanilla ice cream
	For the cake layer
1 cup	flour, more for cake pan
	salt
¼ cup	unsalted butter, more for cake pan and plate
4	eggs
⅔ cup	granulated sugar
1 tsp	vanilla extract
	For the Italian meringue
2¼ cups	granulated sugar, more for sprinkling
1 cup	water
9	egg whites

ORDER OF WORK

1 MAKE THE CAKE

2 MAKE THE STRAWBERRY COULIS

3 PREPARE THE MERINGUE

4 ASSEMBLE AND BAKE THE DESSERT

1 MAKE THE CAKE

1 Heat the oven to 350°F. Butter the cake pan and line the bottom with parchment paper. Butter the paper. Sprinkle in 2 tbsp flour and turn the pan to coat the bottom and sides; turn the pan upside down and tap to remove excess flour.

2 Sift the flour with a pinch of salt. Melt the butter in a small saucepan and let cool.

3 Put the eggs in a large bowl and beat with the electric mixer for a few seconds to mix. Add the sugar and continue beating at high speed until the mixture is pale and thick and leaves a ribbon trail when the beaters are lifted, about 5 minutes. Beat in the vanilla extract.

Eggs and sugar become very pale when beaten

Egg mousse should hold ribbon trail about 3 seconds

ANNE SAYS
"If using a hand whisk, set the bowl over a pan of hot, but not boiling, water and whisk vigorously, about 10 minutes."

4 Sift about one-third of the flour over the egg mixture and fold them together as lightly as possible. Add another third of the flour and fold it in. Fold in the remaining flour and the cooled melted butter.

Paper lining makes cake easy to unmold

5 Pour the batter into the prepared cake pan, then tap the pan on the work surface to level the batter and knock out any air bubbles.

6 Bake in the heated oven until the cake has risen and is just firm to the touch, 30–40 minutes. Run a knife around the edge of the cake and unmold it onto the wire rack. Peel off the lining paper and let the cake cool.

2 MAKE THE STRAWBERRY COULIS

Hulls are easily cut out with point of knife

1 Hull the strawberries with the small knife, washing them only if dirty.

2 Purée the strawberries in the food processor or in a blender, then pour the purée into a bowl.

3 Stir in confectioners' sugar to taste. You should have about 1½ cups of coulis.

3 PREPARE THE MERINGUE

1 Heat the 2¼ cups sugar with the water in a small saucepan until dissolved. Boil without stirring until the syrup reaches the hard ball stage.

2 To test, take the pan from the heat and dip a teaspoon in the hot syrup. Let cool a few seconds; take a little syrup between your finger and thumb. It should form a firm, pliable ball. You can also test the syrup using a candy thermometer; it should register 248°F.

Let syrup cool in spoon before testing with your fingers

Hot syrup cooks egg whites so they make a shiny, stiff meringue

3 While the syrup is boiling, put the egg whites in a bowl and beat with the electric mixer until stiff peaks form when the beaters are lifted, 3–5 minutes. Gradually pour the hot sugar syrup into the egg whites, beating constantly.

ANNE SAYS
"Be sure the syrup is mixed at once into the egg whites or it will solidify on the sides of the bowl."

4 Continue beating the mixture until the meringue is cool and stiff, about 5 minutes.

4 ASSEMBLE AND BAKE THE DESSERT

1 Lightly butter a large heatproof serving plate. Remove the ice cream from the freezer and set aside at room temperature until it is soft enough to scoop.

2 Trim a 1-inch strip from each side of the cake, leaving a 6-inch square piece; reserve the trimmings. Using the serrated knife, split the square of cake horizontally into 2 layers. Set the 2 squares of cake, cut-side up and end to end, on the serving plate to make a long rectangular shape.

Trimmings are reserved to make strawberry cake crumbs

3 Work the reserved cake trimmings in the food processor to form crumbs. Add 1 cup of the strawberry coulis and blend briefly to mix with the cake crumbs.

Two squares of cake are laid side by side to form rectangle

4 Spread the remaining ¹/₂ cup coulis over the cake. Scoop the ice cream into balls and arrange them in a layer on the cake. Scoop and arrange a second layer of ice-cream balls.

ANNE SAYS
"Dip the scoop in warm water to prevent sticking."

5 Quickly smooth the ice-cream layers with the metal spatula to even the surface and edges.

Strawberry cake crumbs form surprise layer between ice cream and meringue

6 Quickly cover the top of the ice-cream layer with the prepared strawberry cake crumbs.

Spoon meringue evenly on top of cake so layer of strawberry cake crumbs remains intact

7 Using a large metal spoon, transfer about half of the meringue to the top of the cake.

Ice cream does not melt if you work quickly

8 Spread the meringue all over the top and sides of the assembled dessert to cover it completely and seal it to the plate.

! TAKE CARE !

The dessert must be completely covered with meringue so the ice cream is insulated from the oven heat.

9 Put the remaining meringue into the pastry bag fitted with the star tube, and pipe a wavy ribbon all around the cake: hold the star tube at an angle, just touching the surface to be decorated so the ribbon sticks to the meringue underneath. Do not lift the tube, but continue piping until all 4 sides of the Alaska have been covered.

Press pastry bag evenly so piped decoration is continuous

10 Pipe lines of double shells along the top edge of the cake: hold the tube at a slight angle, touching the surface. Move the tube forward and then up and down, back toward you, pressing evenly. Do not lift the tube, but continue piping shells, first in one direction, then in another, until the line is complete.

11 Pipe 2 ropes down the center: with the tip of the tube on the surface, pipe a swirl in a clockwise movement. Do not lift the tube, but repeat, making another swirl next to the first. Continue until the rope is complete, then repeat for the second rope. Keep the dessert in the freezer, up to 2 hours.

Add final rope decoration so undercoating of meringue is completely covered

¶❍¶ TO SERVE

Heat the oven to 425°F. Take the dessert from the freezer. Sprinkle the meringue with a little sugar and let stand, 1 minute. Bake in the heated oven until lightly browned, 3–5 minutes. Serve at once, setting the hot serving plate on a tray, if you like.

Fluffy, warm meringue hides surprise of cold ice cream, sponge cake, and fresh strawberry coulis

Tray makes for easy handling of dessert on hot serving plate

V A R I A T I O N

INDIVIDUAL COFFEE BAKED ALASKAS

With individual Baked Alaskas, each diner has the pleasure of spooning through the meringue to the cake and ice cream inside.

1 Omit the strawberries and the confectioners' sugar. Use 1 quart coffee ice cream instead of 1½ quarts vanilla.
2 Bake the cake, trim off the edges, and split horizontally into 2 layers as directed; cut each layer into 4 squares.
3 Put the 8 squares on 2 baking sheets lined with parchment paper. Sprinkle the cake with 1–2 tbsp black coffee.
4 Do not soften the ice cream. Instead, use an ice-cream scoop to shape 8 large balls. Set 1 on each square of cake. Transfer the Alaskas to the freezer.
5 Make the meringue with 1½ cups sugar, ¾ cup water, and 6 egg whites.
6 Pipe flower rosettes of meringue all over the Alaskas, covering the squares of cake and the ice cream completely, and sealing the cakes to the baking sheet. Sprinkle the meringue with sugar and bake as directed.
7 Transfer each Alaska to an individual serving plate and serve immediately. Serves 8.

81

CREPES SUZETTE

EQUIPMENT

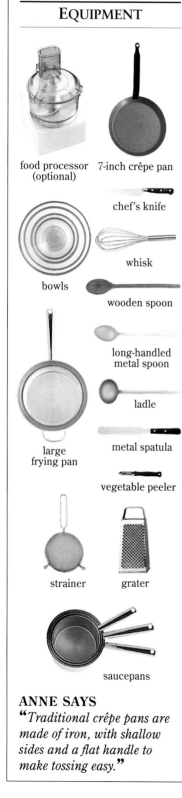

food processor (optional)

7-inch crêpe pan

chef's knife

whisk

bowls

wooden spoon

long-handled metal spoon

ladle

large frying pan

metal spatula

vegetable peeler

strainer

grater

saucepans

ANNE SAYS
"Traditional crêpe pans are made of iron, with shallow sides and a flat handle to make tossing easy."

In this most classic of French desserts, thin crêpes are spread with orange butter, sautéed to caramelize, then flamed just before serving – a sure way to create culinary drama for your guests.

GETTING AHEAD

The crêpes and orange butter can be made up to 3 days ahead. Stack the crêpes, interleaved with wax paper, and store in a plastic bag in the refrigerator (or freeze 2–3 months). Keep the orange butter in the refrigerator, but let it soften 1–2 hours before using. Assemble and flame the crêpes just before serving.

* plus 30 minutes standing time

SHOPPING LIST

For the crêpes	
6 tbsp	unsalted butter, more if needed
1½ cups	flour
1 tbsp	granulated sugar
½ tsp	salt
4	eggs
1½ cups	milk, more if needed
For the orange butter	
¾ cup	unsalted butter, at room temperature
¼ cup	confectioners' sugar
3	large oranges
1 tbsp	Grand Marnier (optional)
For flaming	
⅓ cup	brandy
⅓ cup	Grand Marnier

INGREDIENTS

brandy

oranges

Grand Marnier

milk

granulated sugar

confectioners' sugar

eggs

unsalted butter

flour

ANNE SAYS
"The final number of crêpes varies according to how many you discard when frying."

ORDER OF WORK

1 **MAKE THE CREPE BATTER**

2 **MAKE THE ORANGE BUTTER AND ORANGE JULIENNE**

3 **FRY THE CREPES**

4 **ASSEMBLE AND FLAME THE CREPES**

1 MAKE THE CREPE BATTER

1 Melt the butter in a small saucepan and set aside to cool. Sift the flour into a large bowl. Add the granulated sugar and the salt.

Mix eggs before adding any milk

Try not to incorporate flour into beaten eggs

2 Make a well in the center of the flour and break the eggs into the well. Whisk the eggs just until mixed.

3 Pour half of the milk into the eggs in a slow, steady stream, whisking constantly and gradually drawing in the flour to make a smooth batter.

ANNE SAYS
"If too much liquid is added at this point, the batter will form lumps."

Whisk batter lightly or it will be elastic and then crêpes will be tough

Add milk slowly for smooth batter

4 Gradually whisk in half of the cooled melted butter. Add enough of the remaining milk to give the batter the consistency of thin cream. Cover and let stand, at least 30 minutes. Meanwhile, make the orange butter.

2 MAKE THE ORANGE BUTTER AND ORANGE JULIENNE

1 Put the butter and confectioners' sugar in a bowl and cream them together with the wooden spoon.

2 Finely grate the zest from 2 of the oranges. With the vegetable peeler, pare the zest from the remaining orange; set aside. Cut the pith and skin from all 3 oranges. Slide the knife down both sides of each section to cut it free of the membrane. Reserve orange sections and their juice.

Turn back membrane like pages of a book

Hold orange over bowl to catch juice

3 Add the grated orange zest and 2 tbsp of the reserved orange juice to the butter with the Grand Marnier, if using. Beat until smooth and evenly blended. Cover the bowl and keep the orange butter at room temperature so it does not set.

ANNE SAYS
"Alternatively, you can make the orange butter in the food processor."

Beat vigorously with wooden spoon so orange flavor is released from zest

Finely grated orange zest blends easily with butter

4 Make the orange julienne: cut the pared orange zest lengthwise into the thinnest possible julienne strips. Bring a small pan of cold water to a boil, add the julienne strips, and simmer, 2 minutes. Drain, rinse with cold water, and drain again. Reserve the strips for decoration.

3 FRY THE CREPES

1 If necessary, stir a little more milk into the batter to make it the consistency of thin cream again. Add the remaining melted butter to the crêpe pan and heat gently, then pour the excess butter into a small bowl, leaving a thin film in the pan.

ANNE SAYS
"The batter will have thickened on standing because the grains of starch expand."

2 Reheat the pan, then add a drop of batter to test the temperature of the pan: when the batter spatters briskly, it is hot enough for frying. Stir the batter in the bowl briefly, then quickly ladle a little (2–3 tbsp) into the pan.

! TAKE CARE !
Do not add too much batter or the crêpe will be thick. If too little is added, it will have holes.

Batter will set at once in contact with hot pan

3 Immediately tilt the pan with a twist of the wrist, shaking so the base is evenly covered with batter.

Pan should have only a thin film of butter, otherwise crêpes will be greasy

4 Fry the crêpe over medium-high heat until it is set on top and brown underneath, about 1 minute. Gently loosen the edge of the crêpe with the metal spatula.

5 Turn the crêpe quickly; either slide the metal spatula underneath and flip the crêpe over, or use the fingertips of both hands to turn it. You can also toss the crêpe (see box, below). Continue frying the crêpe over medium-high heat until it is brown on the other side, 30–60 seconds.

ANNE SAYS
"The first crêpe is always a tryout, so don't hesitate to discard any failures."

Frying in butter gives crêpes golden color

6 Slide the crêpe out onto a plate with the side cooked first on top. Continue frying the crêpes, buttering the pan again only when the crêpes start to stick.

ANNE SAYS
"First crêpe after regreasing may be heavy, so discard if necessary."

Lift crêpe with spatula, then flip crêpe over

HOW TO TOSS A CREPE

Crêpes are easier to toss in a non-stick pan, although they brown better in a cast-iron pan.

1 Give the pan a gentle shake to make sure the crêpe is loosened, then toss it up in the air with a quick flip of the wrist.

Sloping sides of pan allow crêpe to be tossed easily

2 When crêpe lands in pan after tossing, slide it to the center of the pan.

4 ASSEMBLE AND FLAME THE CREPES

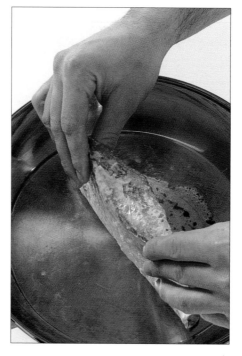

1 Spread the orange butter over the side of each crêpe that was cooked first, stacking the buttered crêpes up again on another plate.

2 Heat the frying pan over medium heat. Add 1 crêpe, orange-butter-side down. Cook briskly until very hot, about 1 minute.

3 Using the metal spatula, fold the crêpe in half and then into quarters to make a triangle.

As crêpes fry, sugar will caramelize and coat bottom of pan, adding a superb flavor

4 Push the folded crêpe to the side of the pan, and add another crêpe, again orange-butter-side down. Continue to fry and fold the crêpes in this way, overlapping them around the side of the pan.

5 Arrange all of the caramelized crêpes in the pan, distributing them evenly.

ANNE SAYS
"If the pan becomes too full, transfer the caramelized crêpes to a plate, cover, and keep them warm while you fry the remaining crêpes."

6 Heat the brandy and Grand Marnier in a small pan, then pour them over the crêpes.

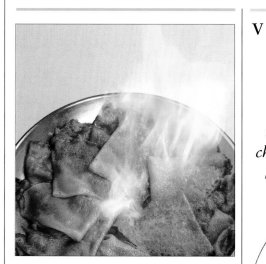

7 Hold a lighted match to the side of the pan to set the alcohol alight. Baste the crêpes with the alcohol until the flames die, 2–3 minutes.

! TAKE CARE !
Flames can rise quite high, so stand back and keep your hair and face away from the pan. Use the long-handled metal spoon for basting.

🍴 TO SERVE
Divide the crêpes among warmed dessert plates and spoon the sauce from the pan over them. Decorate with the orange sections and orange julienne, and serve immediately.

Crêpes Suzette are a spectacular end to any dinner

V A R I A T I O N
CHOCOLATE AND ORANGE CREPES

Cocoa powder in the batter transforms plain crêpes into chocolate ones, making Crêpes Suzette even more delicious.

1 Make the crêpe batter as directed in the main recipe, adding 2 tbsp cocoa powder with the flour.
2 Continue with the dish as directed, sprinkling the crêpes with grated chocolate just before serving.

Orange sections and julienne add a refreshing touch

V A R I A T I O N
APPLE SOUFFLE CREPES

Here, crêpes become cases for airy apple soufflés. Browned, puffed, and dusted with confectioners' sugar, they will crown any special meal.

1 Omit the orange butter, brandy, and Grand Marnier. Make the crêpe batter and fry the crêpes as directed.
2 Core and quarter 2 lb unpeeled tart apples and put them in a saucepan. Add ³/₄ cup water, cover, and cook over low heat until reduced to a pulp, stirring occasionally, 30–45 minutes.
3 Press the pulp through a strainer, then return to the pan. Bring to a boil, stirring, and boil until thick, 5–10 minutes. Stir in 3–4 tbsp brown sugar.
4 Heat the oven to 400°F. Butter 6–8 individual gratin dishes. Whisk 4 egg whites until stiff. Sprinkle in ¹/₄ cup granulated sugar and continue whisking until glossy to make a light meringue, about 20 seconds.
5 If necessary, heat the apple purée until hot to the touch. Stir in 2–3 tbsp Calvados (apple brandy), if you like.
6 Stir one-quarter of the meringue into the apple purée with a rubber spatula. Lightly fold this mixture into the remaining meringue.
7 Put 2–3 tbsp of the apple soufflé mixture on each crêpe. Fold them in half and place in the prepared dishes.
8 Bake the crêpes until puffed and hot, 10–12 minutes. Sprinkle the crêpes with sifted confectioners' sugar, and serve immediately.

APPLE AND ALMOND GALETTES

🍽 SERVES 8 🥄 WORK TIME 25–30 MINUTES 🍲 BAKING TIME 20–30 MINUTES

EQUIPMENT

6-inch pan lid†

thin-bladed knife

melon baller

citrus juicer

pastry brush

small knife

small bowl

vegetable peeler

rolling pin

parchment paper

2 baking sheets

chopping board

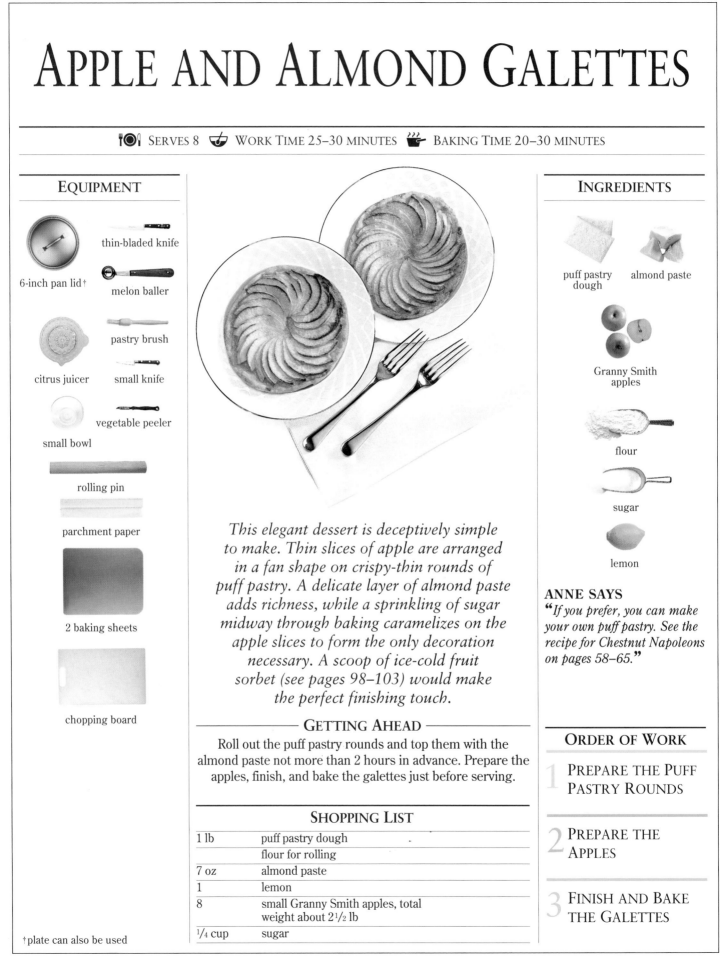

This elegant dessert is deceptively simple to make. Thin slices of apple are arranged in a fan shape on crispy-thin rounds of puff pastry. A delicate layer of almond paste adds richness, while a sprinkling of sugar midway through baking caramelizes on the apple slices to form the only decoration necessary. A scoop of ice-cold fruit sorbet (see pages 98–103) would make the perfect finishing touch.

GETTING AHEAD
Roll out the puff pastry rounds and top them with the almond paste not more than 2 hours in advance. Prepare the apples, finish, and bake the galettes just before serving.

SHOPPING LIST

1 lb	puff pastry dough
	flour for rolling
7 oz	almond paste
1	lemon
8	small Granny Smith apples, total weight about 2½ lb
¼ cup	sugar

INGREDIENTS

puff pastry dough

almond paste

Granny Smith apples

flour

sugar

lemon

ANNE SAYS
"If you prefer, you can make your own puff pastry. See the recipe for Chestnut Napoleons on pages 58–65."

ORDER OF WORK

1 PREPARE THE PUFF PASTRY ROUNDS

2 PREPARE THE APPLES

3 FINISH AND BAKE THE GALETTES

†plate can also be used

1 PREPARE THE PUFF PASTRY ROUNDS

Use light, even strokes, and roll away from you

Dough should roll out like a cloth

1 Lightly flour a work surface. Roll out half of the puff pastry dough to a 14-inch square about 1/8 inch thick.

2 Place the pan lid on the puff pastry dough and, using the lid as a guide, cut out 4 rounds from the pastry dough with the small knife.

3 Sprinkle the baking sheets with water. Set the dough rounds on one of the baking sheets and press them down lightly. Prick each round with a fork in several places, but not near the edge. Repeat with the remaining dough, using the other baking sheet. Chill, 15 minutes.

4 Divide the almond paste into 8 portions and roll each portion into a ball with your hands.

If almond paste sticks, lightly oil your hands

6 Set the round of almond paste on top of a pastry dough round, leaving a 1/2-inch border. Repeat with the remaining almond paste. Refrigerate until ready to bake.

5 Spread a sheet of parchment paper on the work surface. Set 1 ball of almond paste on the paper and cover with another sheet of paper. Roll out the almond paste to a 5-inch round.

Use parchment paper to lift almond paste onto dough rounds

HOW TO HALVE AND CORE AN APPLE

A simple technique like this one can make all the difference to the finished presentation of a pastry.

1 With the point of a small knife, cut around the stem end of the apple; remove the stem. Repeat with the flower end.

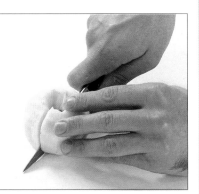

2 With the same knife, cut the apple lengthwise in half.

3 With a melon baller, scoop out the core and seeds from each apple half, leaving as neat a shape as possible. A sharp-edged teaspoon could also be used, but it does not leave such a neat shape.

2 PREPARE THE APPLES

Tart Granny Smith apples have good flavor

1 Cut the lemon in half and squeeze the juice from 1 half into the small bowl. Peel the apples, then halve and core them (see box, left). Rub them with the remaining lemon half to prevent them from turning brown.

2 Set each apple half cut-side down on the chopping board and cut it crosswise into thin slices using the thin-bladed knife. As the apples are sliced, brush them with lemon juice.

3 FINISH AND BAKE THE GALETTES

1 Heat the oven to 425°F. Arrange the apple slices, overlapping them slightly, in a ring on the almond paste rounds, covering them completely. Leave a thin border of puff pastry dough around the edge.

2 Bake the apple and almond galettes until the pastry edges have risen around the almond paste and are light golden, 15–20 minutes. Sprinkle the apples evenly with the sugar.

3 Return the apple and almond galettes to the oven and continue baking until the apples are golden brown, caramelized around the edges, and just tender when tested with the tip of the small knife, 5–10 minutes.

ANNE SAYS
"Caramelized sugar should outline the edges of the apple slices, and there may be some unmelted sugar left on top of the galettes."

🍴 **TO SERVE**
Transfer the galettes to warmed individual serving plates and serve at once.

Apple slices are arranged in pretty flower pattern

Crisp pastry is perfect foil for sweet almond paste and tart apples

RHUBARB GALETTES

Sticks of rhubarb arranged like the spokes of a wheel on top of puff pastry rounds replace sliced apples in these galettes. The pastry rounds have a hole cut in the center, making a perfect spot for scoops of vanilla ice cream. Melted red currant jelly brushed over galettes just before serving makes rhubarb glisten.

1 Omit the apples and almond paste. Peel the tough strings from 1 lb rhubarb with a vegetable peeler. Cut the rhubarb into thin sticks 1½ inches long.

2 Put the sticks of rhubarb in a bowl and sprinkle with ⅓ cup sugar. Cover with a plate that fits inside the bowl, set a weight on top, and let stand to extract the juice, about 45 minutes.
3 Meanwhile, prepare the puff pastry rounds as directed, but do not prick them. With a 2-inch round cookie cutter, cut a hole out of the center of each pastry dough round.
4 Heat the oven to 450°F. Drain the rhubarb thoroughly and pat dry with paper towels. Arrange the sticks in a single layer on the pastry dough rounds like the spokes of a wheel.
5 Bake the galettes in the heated oven until the pastry has risen and is light golden, about 10–15 minutes. Sprinkle with ⅓ cup sugar and bake until caramelized, 3–5 minutes longer.
6 Meanwhile, melt ½ cup red currant jelly in a small pan.
7 Brush the melted jelly over the galettes and transfer them to warmed individual plates. Serve topped with vanilla ice cream, if you like.

GRAND MARNIER SOUFFLE

EQUIPMENT

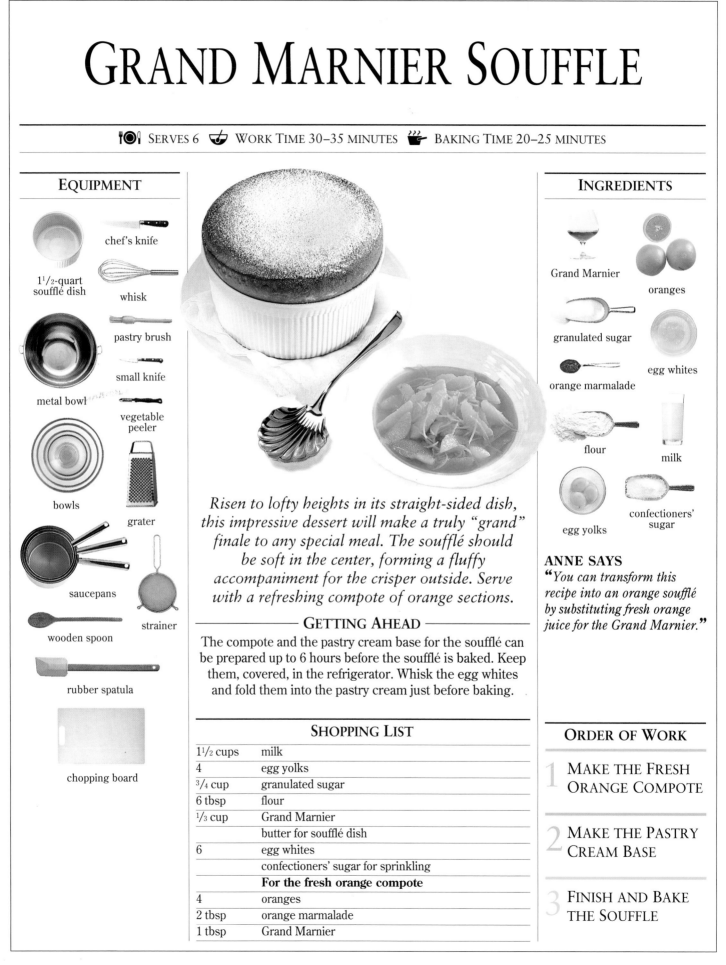

- chef's knife
- 1¹/₂-quart soufflé dish
- whisk
- pastry brush
- small knife
- metal bowl
- vegetable peeler
- bowls
- grater
- saucepans
- strainer
- wooden spoon
- rubber spatula
- chopping board

INGREDIENTS

- Grand Marnier
- oranges
- granulated sugar
- egg whites
- orange marmalade
- flour
- milk
- egg yolks
- confectioners' sugar

Risen to lofty heights in its straight-sided dish, this impressive dessert will make a truly "grand" finale to any special meal. The soufflé should be soft in the center, forming a fluffy accompaniment for the crisper outside. Serve with a refreshing compote of orange sections.

GETTING AHEAD
The compote and the pastry cream base for the soufflé can be prepared up to 6 hours before the soufflé is baked. Keep them, covered, in the refrigerator. Whisk the egg whites and fold them into the pastry cream just before baking.

ANNE SAYS
"You can transform this recipe into an orange soufflé by substituting fresh orange juice for the Grand Marnier."

SHOPPING LIST

1¹/₂ cups	milk
4	egg yolks
³/₄ cup	granulated sugar
6 tbsp	flour
¹/₃ cup	Grand Marnier
	butter for soufflé dish
6	egg whites
	confectioners' sugar for sprinkling
	For the fresh orange compote
4	oranges
2 tbsp	orange marmalade
1 tbsp	Grand Marnier

ORDER OF WORK

1 MAKE THE FRESH ORANGE COMPOTE

2 MAKE THE PASTRY CREAM BASE

3 FINISH AND BAKE THE SOUFFLE

1 MAKE THE FRESH ORANGE COMPOTE

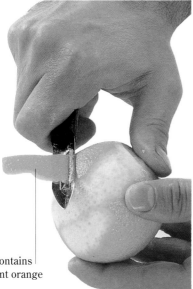

Zest contains fragrant orange oils

1 With the vegetable peeler, pare the zest from one of the oranges, taking care not to include any of the bitter white pith.

2 Using the chef's knife, cut the zest lengthwise into the finest possible julienne strips.

3 Bring a small saucepan of water to a boil. Add the julienne strips and simmer, 2 minutes. Drain, rinse under cold running water, and drain again. Transfer the strips to a bowl.

4 Finely grate the zest from a second orange into a dish and reserve for the soufflé.

Zest trapped in teeth of grater can be removed with stiff brush

HOW TO PEEL AND SECTION CITRUS FRUIT

Seedless citrus fruit, such as navel oranges, are the most suitable for cutting into sections.

1 With a chef's knife, cut away both ends of the citrus fruit just to the flesh. Set the fruit upright on a chopping board. Working from top to bottom, cut away the zest, pith, and skin, following the curve of the fruit.

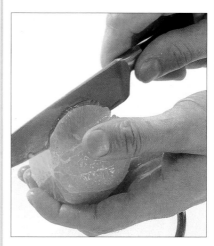

2 Holding the fruit over a bowl, slide the knife down one side of a section, cutting the section from the membrane. Cut down the other side and pull out the section. Repeat with the remaining sections, turning back the flaps of membrane like the pages of a book.

ANNE SAYS
"Squeeze the leftover membrane over the bowl to catch the juice."

5 Section all 4 oranges (see box, page 93), working over a bowl to catch the juice. Add the orange sections to the julienne strips of zest.

Marmalade helps thicken fresh orange compote

Marmalade mixture is cool when added to orange

6 Put the juice from sectioning the oranges and the marmalade in a small saucepan. Heat gently until the marmalade has melted, stirring occasionally. Remove from the heat and let cool slightly.

7 Add the marmalade mixture to the orange sections and julienne, and stir to mix. Stir in the Grand Marnier. Cover, and chill until ready to serve.

2 MAKE THE PASTRY CREAM BASE

Stir in milk slowly to avoid lumps

1 Scald the milk, bringing it just to a boil in a saucepan. Meanwhile, whisk the egg yolks with three-quarters of the granulated sugar until thick and light colored, 2–3 minutes.

2 Stir in the flour with the whisk. Then gradually stir in the hot milk until the mixture is smooth.

3 Pour the pastry cream back into the saucepan. Bring to a boil over medium heat, whisking constantly until it thickens.

! TAKE CARE !
If lumps form, remove from the heat at once and whisk until the cream is smooth again.

Stir in liqueur thoroughly until mixture is smooth again

Use whisk to blend in orange zest and liqueur

4 Reduce the heat to low and cook the pastry cream, still whisking constantly, until it softens slightly, about 2 minutes.

ANNE SAYS
"This will ensure that the flour is completely cooked."

5 Remove the pan from the heat. Add the reserved grated orange zest and the Grand Marnier, and stir in with the whisk.

3 FINISH AND BAKE THE SOUFFLE

Sugar stiffens egg whites

2 Whisk the egg whites in the metal bowl until stiff. Sprinkle in the remaining granulated sugar and continue whisking until a glossy light meringue, about 20 seconds. Fold the meringue and pastry cream base together (see box, page 96).

1 Heat the oven to 400°F. Brush the inside of the soufflé dish generously with butter. If necessary, reheat the pastry cream until hot to the touch.

HOW TO CUT AND FOLD MIXTURES TOGETHER

Two mixtures can be folded together more easily if their consistency is similar. If one ingredient is much lighter or more liquid than the other, such as the meringue and pastry cream base here, first thoroughly stir a little of the lighter mixture into the heavier one to soften it.

Rubber spatula is ideal for transferring mixture to bowl

1 Spoon one-quarter of the light mixture over the heavier one and stir until thoroughly incorporated, using a rubber spatula or a wooden or metal spoon.

2 Pour this mixture into the remaining light mixture in the large bowl.

3 With the rubber spatula or spoon, cut down into the center of the bowl, scoop under the contents, and turn them over in a rolling motion. At the same time, with your other hand, slowly turn the bowl counter-clockwise.

ANNE SAYS
"This should be a synchronized movement: cut and scoop with the spatula in one hand, turn the bowl with the other. With this method, the spatula reaches the maximum volume of mixture in one movement, so the mixture is folded quickly and loses a minimum of air."

Cut down into center of mixture with edge of spatula

Scoop under contents of bowl and bring spatula up, turning bowl counter-clockwise

4 Continue gently folding the mixtures together until they are thoroughly combined.

3 Gently pour the souffle mixture into the prepared dish, cleaning out the bowl with the rubber spatula. Tap the dish on the table to eliminate any large pockets of air.

ANNE SAYS
"The souffle mixture should fill the dish to within ³/₈ inch of the rim."

After folding in egg whites, mixture should remain quite stiff

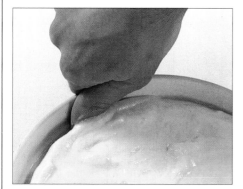

4 Smooth the top of the mixture, then run your thumb around the edge of the dish to make a shallow indentation at the side of the souffle. Place the souffle in the oven and bake until puffed and brown, 20–25 minutes.

ANNE SAYS
"When gently shaken, the souffle should be firm on the outside but still slightly soft in the center."

🍴 **TO SERVE**
Sift confectioners' sugar over the top of the souffle, working quickly as the souffle will lose volume within minutes as it cools. Serve at once, with the fresh orange compote in a bowl.

Golden souffle is firm on outside and soft in center

Tangy orange compote contrasts beautifully with creamy souffle

V A R I A T I O N

HOT COFFEE SOUFFLE

Classic coffee souffle takes an innovative turn with a flavoring of cardamom, echoing Turkish coffee.

1 Omit the fresh orange compote. Instead, put 1½ cups light cream in a saucepan and add 2 lightly crushed cardamom pods. Bring just to a boil.
2 Remove from the heat, cover, and leave to infuse, 10–15 minutes. When the cream is cool, strain it and chill, covered, until serving.
3 For the pastry cream base, add ¼ cup coarsely ground coffee to the milk before heating, then remove from the heat, cover, and set aside in a warm place to infuse, 10–15 minutes.
4 Whisk the egg yolks, sugar, and flour as directed in the main recipe, then strain in the hot flavored milk. Continue with the pastry cream base as directed, omitting the orange zest and replacing the Grand Marnier with Tia Maria or Kahlúa.
5 Butter the souffle dish. Finish and bake the souffle as directed.
6 Quickly sift cocoa powder over the top of the souffle and serve immediately, with the spiced cardamom cream as a sauce.

TRIO OF SORBETS

†Ⓞ¶ SERVES 8   ⏱ WORK TIME 40–50 MINUTES   ❄ FREEZING TIME 6 HOURS*

EQUIPMENT

chef's knife

small knife

vegetable peeler

food processor †

slotted spoon

citrus juicer

ladle

wooden spoon

conical strainer

ice-cream maker

chopping board

bowls

saucepans

rubber spatula

†blender can also be used

INGREDIENTS

peaches

pears

raspberries

lemons

sugar

Poire Williams liqueur

fresh mint sprigs

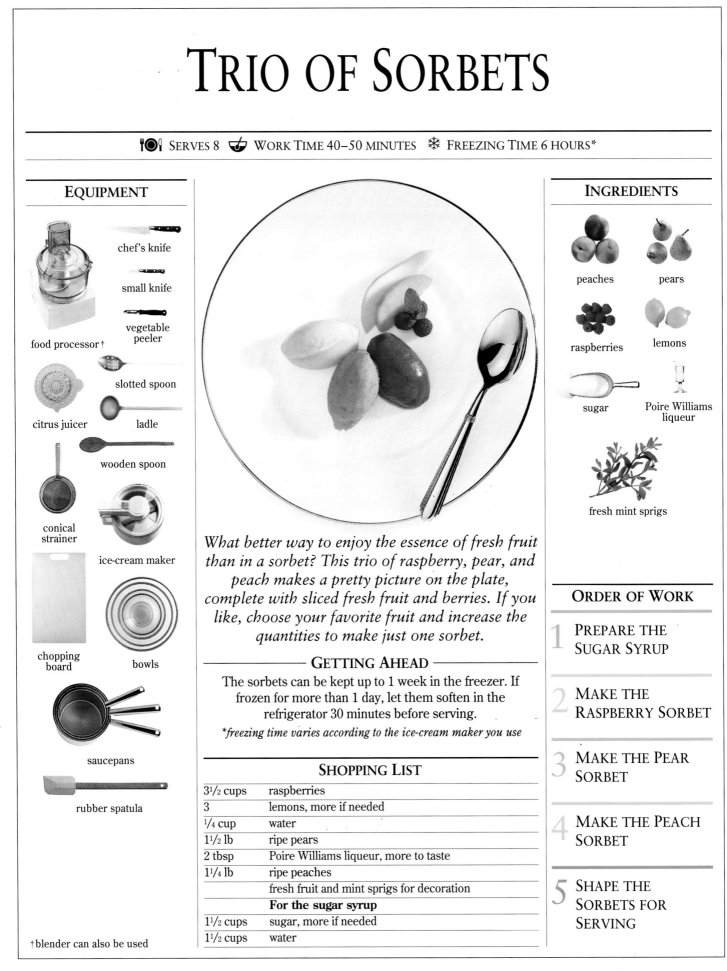

What better way to enjoy the essence of fresh fruit than in a sorbet? This trio of raspberry, pear, and peach makes a pretty picture on the plate, complete with sliced fresh fruit and berries. If you like, choose your favorite fruit and increase the quantities to make just one sorbet.

GETTING AHEAD

The sorbets can be kept up to 1 week in the freezer. If frozen for more than 1 day, let them soften in the refrigerator 30 minutes before serving.

*freezing time varies according to the ice-cream maker you use

SHOPPING LIST

3¹/₂ cups	raspberries
3	lemons, more if needed
¹/₄ cup	water
1¹/₂ lb	ripe pears
2 tbsp	Poire Williams liqueur, more to taste
1¹/₄ lb	ripe peaches
	fresh fruit and mint sprigs for decoration
	For the sugar syrup
1¹/₂ cups	sugar, more if needed
1¹/₂ cups	water

ORDER OF WORK

1 PREPARE THE SUGAR SYRUP

2 MAKE THE RASPBERRY SORBET

3 MAKE THE PEAR SORBET

4 MAKE THE PEACH SORBET

5 SHAPE THE SORBETS FOR SERVING

1 PREPARE THE SUGAR SYRUP

1 Combine the sugar and water in a medium saucepan and heat until the sugar has dissolved.

2 Bring to a boil, and boil without stirring until the syrup is clear, 2–3 minutes. Pour the sugar syrup into a measuring cup and let cool completely.

2 MAKE THE RASPBERRY SORBET

1 Pick over the raspberries, washing them only if they are dirty. Purée them in the food processor.

Food processor is ideal for puréeing berries, but blender can also be used

2 Work the raspberry purée through the strainer held over a bowl, to remove the raspberry seeds. There should be ³/₄ cup purée. If necessary, purée a few more berries.

3 Squeeze the juice from the lemons; there should be just over ¹/₂ cup. Keep the squeezed lemon halves.

4 Add the water, 2 tbsp of the lemon juice, and one-third of the sugar syrup to the bowl of raspberry purée. Taste, and stir in more lemon juice or sugar if needed. Chill until cold, then taste again.

ANNE SAYS
"The taste of a frozen mixture is blunted by the cold, so be sure the flavors are concentrated."

5 Pour the raspberry mixture into the ice-cream maker and freeze until firm, following the manufacturer's directions. Meanwhile, chill a bowl in the freezer.

6 Transfer the raspberry sorbet to the chilled bowl. Cover it and freeze at least 4 hours to allow the flavor to mellow. Meanwhile, make the pear and peach sorbets.

Be sure purée is cold before pouring it into freezing container

3 MAKE THE PEAR SORBET

1 Pour half of the remaining sugar syrup into a small saucepan and add 2 tbsp of the lemon juice.

When coring pears, scoop out tough stem as well

2 Peel the pears with the vegetable peeler, then cut out the flower and stem ends with the small knife. Cut each pear in half, then into quarters, and cut out the core.

Pear will not discolor when rubbed with lemon

3 Rub the pear quarters with the squeezed lemon halves so that they do not discolor.

4 Cut the pear quarters into chunks and drop them immediately into the saucepan of syrup.

5 Bring to a boil, then simmer the pears until soft and translucent, 5–10 minutes depending on ripeness.

6 Purée the pears with their syrup in the food processor, or purée them in 2 batches in a blender.

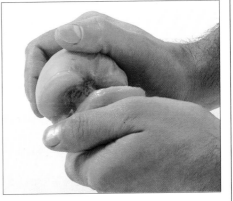

Small ladle is best for pressing purée through strainer

7 Work the purée through the strainer held over a bowl. There should be nearly 2 cups pear purée. Stir in the liqueur, and taste, adding more liqueur, lemon juice, or sugar if needed. Freeze the pear sorbet as for the raspberry sorbet.

4 MAKE THE PEACH SORBET

1 Immerse the peaches in a pan of boiling water, 10–20 seconds depending on their ripeness. Transfer them to a bowl of cold water with the slotted spoon. Cut each peach in half.

Use indentation on one side of peach as guide for cutting

2 Using both hands, give a quick sharp twist to each peach half to loosen it from the pit. Lift or scoop out the pit with the knife and discard it.

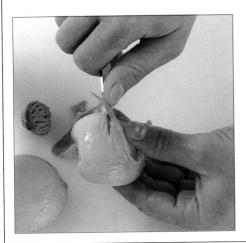

3 With the small knife, peel the skin from the peach halves.

4 Using the chef's knife, cut the skinned peach halves into chunks.

Use knife with stainless steel blade so fruit does not discolor

5 Put the peach chunks into the food processor and add the remaining sugar syrup and lemon juice.

Fruit is cut into chunks so it purées quickly

Food processor is used here for puréeing but blender can also be used

6 Purée until smooth. There should be nearly 2 cups purée. Taste the purée, and add more lemon juice or sugar if needed. Freeze the peach sorbet as for the raspberry sorbet.

5 SHAPE THE SORBETS FOR SERVING

1 Chill a baking sheet lined with parchment paper in the freezer. Soften the sorbets slightly in the refrigerator, if necessary. Dip 2 tablespoons in cold water and use one to scoop out a generous spoonful of sorbet. Use the second spoon to shape the oval, then let the oval fall onto the chilled baking sheet. Repeat for the remaining sorbet. Place in the freezer until the sorbet hardens, 1/2–1 hour.

Fruit garnish hints at flavor of sorbets

🍴 TO SERVE
Just before serving, lift the scoops off the paper and arrange one of each flavor on each of 8 chilled dessert plates. Garnish the plates with fresh fruit and mint sprigs, and serve immediately.

Plate is chilled so sorbet does not melt

V A R I A T I O N
PANACHE OF SORBETS

Here is a selection of different-flavored sorbets for you to try. Strawberry Sorbet is topped with the perfect finishing touch – chocolate-dipped strawberries. Apple and Calvados Sorbet is full of flavor from tart apples and a touch of apple brandy. Tangerine Sorbet is tangy and refreshing, an ideal dessert to follow a rich main dish.

Strawberry Sorbet

1 Omit the raspberries, pears, Poire Williams liqueur, peaches, and all but ½ lemon. Make the sugar syrup as directed, using 1 cup sugar and 1 cup water. Let cool completely.
2 Pick over 1½ pints strawberries, washing them only if they are dirty. Hull the berries and halve or quarter them if they are large.
3 Combine the strawberries, sugar syrup, and the juice of ½ lemon in a food processor. Purée until smooth. Taste the purée, and add more lemon juice or sugar if needed.
4 Freeze the sorbet in the ice-cream maker as directed.
5 Scoop balls of sorbet into stemmed dessert glasses and top each serving with a strawberry that has been dipped in melted chocolate. Serves 6.

Apple and Calvados Sorbet

1 Omit the raspberries, pears, Poire Williams liqueur, peaches, and all but ½ lemon. Make the sugar syrup as directed, using 1 cup sugar and 1 cup water. Let cool completely.
2 Peel 3 lb tart apples with a vegetable peeler. With a small knife, cut the flower and stem ends from the apples. Cut them in half and then into quarters. Cut out the cores. Rub the apple quarters with the lemon half so they do not discolor.
3 Continue as directed for the pear sorbet, adding 2 tbsp Calvados in place of the Poire Williams.
4 Scoop small balls of the sorbet into shallow coupe glasses. If you like, add a spoonful of Calvados to each glass and a crisp cookie. Serves 6.

Tangerine Sorbet

1 Omit the raspberries, pears, Poire Williams liqueur, peaches, and all but 1 lemon. Make the sugar syrup as directed, using 1 cup sugar and 1 cup water. Let cool completely.
2 Squeeze the juice from 10–12 tangerines; there should be 2 cups juice. Stir the juice into the sugar syrup with the juice of the lemon. Freeze as directed for the raspberry sorbet.
3 Scoop the sorbet into stemmed dessert glasses. Garnish each with tangerine slices and add a crisp cookie, if you like. Serves 6.

AMARETTI AND CHOCOLATE BOMBE

🍽 SERVES 8–10 🥄 WORK TIME 40–60 MINUTES ❄ FREEZING TIME 10–11 HOURS

EQUIPMENT

2-quart bombe mold with lid †

ice-cream maker

electric mixer

pastry bag fitted with star tube

thick plastic bag

bowls

parchment paper

strainer

saucepans

vegetable peeler

wooden spoon

small knife

rolling pin

metal spatula

grater

large metal spoon

chef's knife

whisk

rubber spatula

candy thermometer (optional)

† deep metal bowl can also be used

An ice-cream bombe, with its attractive shape and contrasting center, always heralds festivity. Here, Amaretto ice cream surrounds an Amaretti and chocolate filling. It's a favorite of mine because it can be prepared ahead with only the decoration and chocolate sauce to be made before serving.

INGREDIENTS

semisweet chocolate

egg yolks

Amaretto liqueur

sugar

milk

heavy cream

Amaretti cookies

cornstarch

SHOPPING LIST

For the Amaretto ice cream	
2 ½ cups	milk
10 tbsp	sugar
8	egg yolks
2 tbsp	cornstarch
3 tbsp	Amaretto liqueur
1 cup	heavy cream
For the chocolate bombe filling	
½ cup	sugar
½ cup	water
4	egg yolks
½ cup	heavy cream
4 oz	semisweet chocolate
18	small Amaretti cookies, total weight about 3 ½ oz
For the warm chocolate sauce	
8 oz	semisweet chocolate
¾ cup	water
For the decoration	
¾ cup	heavy cream
1 oz	semisweet chocolate

ORDER OF WORK

1 MAKE THE AMARETTO ICE CREAM

2 MAKE THE CHOCOLATE FILLING AND FREEZE THE BOMBE

3 MAKE THE WARM CHOCOLATE SAUCE

4 UNMOLD AND DECORATE THE BOMBE

1 MAKE THE AMARETTO ICE CREAM

1 Put the milk in a medium saucepan and bring just to a boil. Remove the saucepan from the heat, set aside one-quarter of the milk, and add the sugar to the remainder. Stir until the sugar has dissolved.

2 Put the egg yolks and cornstarch in a medium bowl. Using the whisk, blend them together until smooth and evenly combined.

3 Pour the sweetened milk into the egg yolk mixture, whisking just until evenly blended.

4 Return the mixture to the pan and cook over medium heat, stirring constantly, until the custard comes just to a boil and thickens enough to coat the back of the spoon. Remove the saucepan from the heat.

ANNE SAYS
"Cornstarch helps prevent the custard from curdling."

When custard has thickened, your finger will leave a clear trail across spoon

Custard should be smooth and creamy

5 Stir the reserved milk into the custard. Strain the custard into a bowl and let cool completely.

6 If a skin has formed on the custard, whisk to dissolve it, then whisk in the Amaretto liqueur.

7 Pour the cooled custard into the ice-cream maker and freeze it until it becomes slushy, following the manufacturer's directions.

Custard should be half frozen before cream is added

Ice-cream maker will mix cream into custard

8 Pour the cream into a chilled bowl and whip until it forms soft peaks and just holds a shape.

9 Add the whipped cream to the half-frozen custard and continue freezing until the ice cream is firm but still soft enough to spread. Meanwhile, chill the bombe mold in the freezer.

10 Spoon the ice cream into the bombe mold and spread it over the bottom and sides in an even layer 1½ inches thick.

11 Make a neat, even hollow in the center of the ice cream. Cover and freeze until firm, ½–1 hour. Meanwhile, make the bombe filling.

ANNE SAYS
"You can use either a classic, plain bombe mold or a decorative mold for this dessert."

Use back of spoon to smooth hollow in ice cream

2 MAKE THE CHOCOLATE FILLING AND FREEZE THE BOMBE

2 While the syrup is boiling, lightly beat the egg yolks in a large bowl just until mixed.

1 Put the sugar and water in a small saucepan and heat until dissolved, stirring occasionally. Boil without stirring until the syrup reaches the soft ball stage. To test, take the pan from the heat and dip a teaspoon in the hot syrup. Let the syrup cool a few seconds, then take a little between your finger and thumb; it should form a soft ball. If using a candy thermometer, it should register 239°F.

Electric mixer makes light work of whisking, but hand whisk can also be used

3 Gradually pour the hot sugar syrup into the yolks, beating constantly with the electric mixer or with a hand whisk.

Add syrup to egg yolks while still very hot

4 Continue beating at high speed until the mixture is cool, very thick, and pale, about 5 minutes.

Folded dish towel holds bowl steady as you whisk

5 Pour the cream into a chilled bowl and whip until it forms soft peaks and just holds a shape.

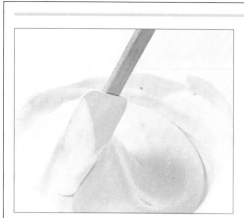

7 Grate the chocolate: holding the bar of chocolate with a piece of parchment paper or foil, work it against the coarsest grid of the grater.

6 Add the whipped cream to the egg yolk mousse and fold the mixtures together: cut down into the center of the bowl, scoop under the contents, and turn them over in a rolling motion. At the same time, with your other hand, turn the bowl counter-clockwise.

! TAKE CARE !
Be sure the mousse is cool before adding the cream.

If chocolate is chilled before using, it will not melt when grated

8 Put 7–8 of the Amaretti cookies in the plastic bag and crumble them coarsely by pounding with the rolling pin. Reserve the remaining Amaretti cookies for decoration.

ANNE SAYS
"The number of cookies needed for the decoration depends on the width or size of your bombe mold."

9 Add the grated chocolate and the crumbled Amaretti cookies to the bombe mixture, and fold in until thoroughly incorporated.

Rubber spatula is ideal utensil for folding ingredients into delicate bombe mixture

10 Remove the ice-cream-lined mold from the freezer and spoon in the bombe filling. Smooth the top with the metal spatula.

Protect bombe with parchment paper before adding metal lid

11 Cover with parchment paper and the lid or a piece of foil and freeze until very firm, at least 8 hours.

3 MAKE THE WARM CHOCOLATE SAUCE

1 Cut the chocolate into large chunks. Chop them with the chef's knife, or in a food processor using the pulse button.

Check consistency of sauce by lifting spoonful out of pan

Warm chocolate sauce should be rich but easy to pour

2 Combine the chocolate and water in a small saucepan and stir over gentle heat until the chocolate is melted and the sauce is smooth.

3 Simmer until the sauce is slightly thickened, with the consistency of thin cream, 2–3 minutes. Remove the sauce from the heat and keep warm.

4 UNMOLD AND DECORATE THE BOMBE

1 Remove the lid or foil and dip the mold in a bowl of cool water, 30–60 seconds. Lift it out and wipe dry.

2 Run the small knife around the edge of the mold to loosen the bombe. Peel off the parchment paper.

Damp cloth will help loosen bombe from mold

Serving plate should be chilled or bombe may melt

3 Set a chilled serving plate on top of the mold. Holding them together, turn them over. Wrap a damp cloth around the mold for a few moments, then lift it off. Wipe the plate to remove any melted ice cream. Keep the bombe in the freezer until serving.

HOW TO PIPE CREAM DECORATIONS

A large star piping tube is used for piping decorations of whipped cream, which add a professional finish to any dessert.

For a flower rosette: hold the tube upright and not quite touching the surface to be decorated. Press the bag until the flower rosette is the size wanted, then stop pressing as you lift the tube upward.

For a rope of double shells: hold the tube at a slight angle, touching the surface to be decorated. To pipe a shell, move the tube forward and then up and down, back toward you, pressing evenly. Do not lift the tube, but continue piping shells, first in one direction, then in another, until the rope is completed.

For a swirled rosette: hold the tube near the surface to be decorated. Pressing evenly, move the tube in a tight circle to form the rosette. Stop pressing before lifting the tube. To make a border of swirled rosettes, start and stop each rosette in the same place and make them all clockwise or counter-clockwise.

Top of pastry bag is twisted so no air is left in

4 For the decoration, scrape fine shavings from the chocolate with the vegetable peeler. Whip the cream in a chilled bowl until stiff peaks form; put it into the pastry bag fitted with the star tube. Press a reserved cookie on the edge of the bombe. Pipe a cream rosette or other decorative shape (see box, page 110) next to the cookie. Continue all around the bombe to make a border. Sprinkle each rosette with chocolate shavings.

⦿| TO SERVE
Serve the bombe immediately with the warm chocolate sauce. Cut the bombe into wedges at the table.

VARIATION
SPICED HONEY AND CHERRY BOMBE

In this deliciously different bombe, a smooth, rich honey ice cream spiced with cardamom makes an intriguing contrast to the filling of lightly poached fresh cherries. A garnet-hued cherry sauce is the perfect accompaniment to the bombe.

1 Omit the chocolate sauce.
2 To make spiced honey ice cream, omit the sugar and Amaretto liqueur from the main recipe for Amaretto ice cream. Put the milk in a saucepan and add the seeds from 5 cardamom pods. Bring just to a boil, then remove from the heat, cover, and let stand in a warm place, 10–15 minutes.
3 Put the egg yolks and cornstarch in a bowl and add $2/3$ cup clear flower honey. Whisk until smooth and evenly blended. Strain in three-quarters of the spiced milk, whisking constantly. Continue making the ice cream as directed, then freeze. When firm but spreadable, line the bombe mold.

4 Make the bombe filling as directed, but replace the chocolate and Amaretti cookies with cherries: pit $1^{1}/_{2}$ lb Bing or other sweet cherries using a cherry pitter or the point of a vegetable peeler. Put them in a saucepan with $1/4$ cup sugar, cover, and cook over low heat, stirring, until the juice runs from the fruit and the sugar is dissolved, 5–10 minutes. Let cool, then drain the cherries in a strainer set over another saucepan. Add one-third of the cherries to the bombe mixture; reserve the remainder and the cherry juice. Finish and freeze the bombe as directed.
5 To make the cherry sauce, bring the cherry juice to a boil. Simmer gently until slightly reduced and thickened, 3–5 minutes. Return the remaining cherries to the juice and add a squeeze of lemon juice and sugar to taste. Let the sauce cool.
6 Unmold the bombe as directed and serve with the cherry sauce.

Amaretto ice cream conceals a surprise chocolate and almond-cookie filling

— **GETTING AHEAD** —
The bombe can be made up to 1 week ahead and frozen. Make the sauce and unmold the bombe not more than 1 hour before serving.

ICED PEACH SOUFFLE

🍽 SERVES 6–8 🥄 WORK TIME 30–40 MINUTES ❄ FREEZING TIME 6 HOURS

EQUIPMENT

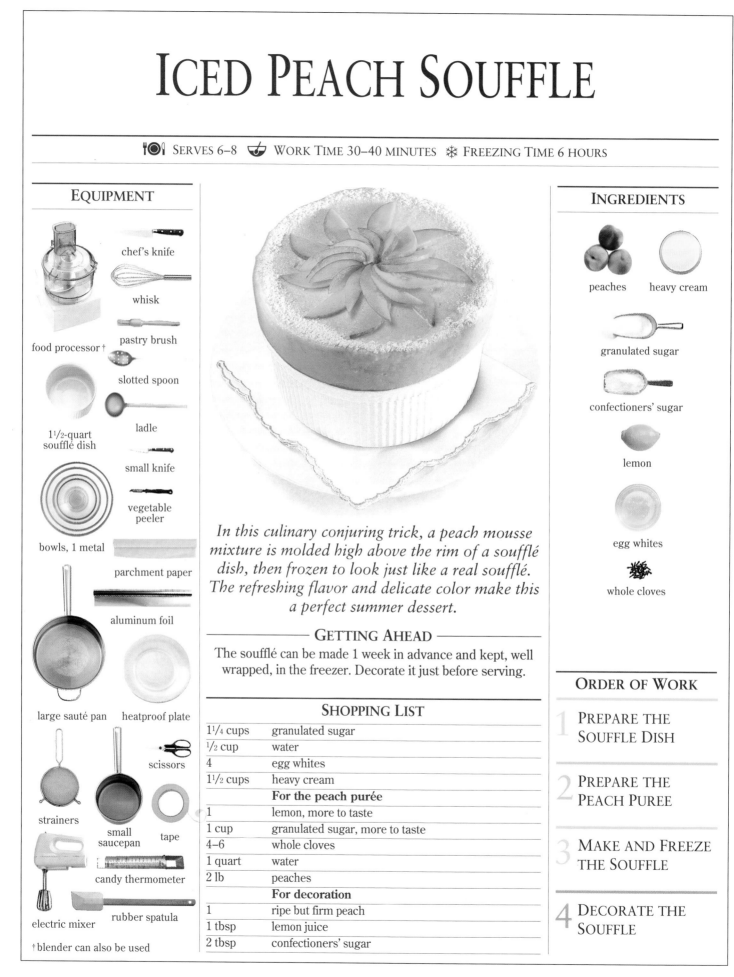

- chef's knife
- whisk
- pastry brush
- food processor †
- slotted spoon
- 1½-quart soufflé dish
- ladle
- small knife
- vegetable peeler
- bowls, 1 metal
- parchment paper
- aluminum foil
- large sauté pan
- heatproof plate
- scissors
- strainers
- small saucepan
- tape
- electric mixer
- candy thermometer
- rubber spatula

† blender can also be used

INGREDIENTS

- peaches
- heavy cream
- granulated sugar
- confectioners' sugar
- lemon
- egg whites
- whole cloves

In this culinary conjuring trick, a peach mousse mixture is molded high above the rim of a soufflé dish, then frozen to look just like a real soufflé. The refreshing flavor and delicate color make this a perfect summer dessert.

GETTING AHEAD

The soufflé can be made 1 week in advance and kept, well wrapped, in the freezer. Decorate it just before serving.

SHOPPING LIST

1¼ cups	granulated sugar
½ cup	water
4	egg whites
1½ cups	heavy cream
	For the peach purée
1	lemon, more to taste
1 cup	granulated sugar, more to taste
4–6	whole cloves
1 quart	water
2 lb	peaches
	For decoration
1	ripe but firm peach
1 tbsp	lemon juice
2 tbsp	confectioners' sugar

ORDER OF WORK

1. PREPARE THE SOUFFLE DISH

2. PREPARE THE PEACH PUREE

3. MAKE AND FREEZE THE SOUFFLE

4. DECORATE THE SOUFFLE

1 PREPARE THE SOUFFLE DISH

1 Cut a piece of foil 2 inches longer than the circumference of the soufflé dish. Fold it lengthwise in half and wrap it around the dish. It should stand at least 3 inches above the rim.

2 Secure the foil "collar" with adhesive tape. Chill the prepared dish in the freezer while you make the soufflé.

2 PREPARE THE PEACH PUREE

2 With the small knife, cut each peach in half using the indentation on one side as a guide. Using both hands, twist sharply to loosen each half from the pit. Discard the pit.

Use tip of knife to scoop out pit

1 With the vegetable peeler, pare the zest from the lemon. Squeeze the juice and reserve it. Combine the lemon zest, sugar, cloves, and water in the sauté pan. Heat gently, stirring occasionally, until the sugar has dissolved, then boil without stirring, 2 minutes. Remove from the heat.

Make sure peach halves fit in pan in one layer

3 Stir the reserved lemon juice into the syrup. Immerse the peach halves immediately in the hot syrup, cut-side up.

Set peaches cut-side up because rounded side would float above surface of syrup

4 Cover the peach halves with a round of parchment paper and set the heatproof plate on top of them to keep them submerged.

5 Return the pan to the heat and poach the peaches gently until just tender, 10–15 minutes. Take from the heat and remove the peaches with the slotted spoon. When cool enough to handle, peel the peach halves with the small knife.

Test peaches by piercing with point of small knife

6 Strain, and reserve ½ cup poaching syrup. Purée the peaches with the reserved syrup in the food processor; there should be 2 cups purée. Taste the purée and add more sugar or lemon juice if necessary. Keep the purée cool.

3 MAKE AND FREEZE THE SOUFFLE

1 Heat the sugar with the water in the saucepan until dissolved. Boil without stirring until the syrup reaches the hard ball stage (248°F on a candy thermometer). To test, take the pan from the heat, dip a teaspoon in the syrup, and let it cool a few seconds. Take a little syrup between your finger and thumb. It should form a firm, pliable ball.

2 While the syrup is boiling, beat the egg whites in the metal bowl with the hand whisk or electric mixer until stiff peaks form when the whisk is lifted. Gradually pour the hot sugar syrup into the whisked egg whites, beating constantly.

3 Continue beating until the mixture is cool and forms a stiff meringue, about 5 minutes.

5 Add the peach purée to the meringue and fold together: cut down into the center of the bowl with the rubber spatula, scoop under the contents, and turn them over in a rolling motion. At the same time, with the other hand, turn the bowl counter-clockwise. Fold in the whipped cream.

Meringue and peach purée must be cool when folded together

4 Pour the cream into a chilled bowl and whip until soft peaks form and it just holds a shape.

6 Ladle the mixture into the prepared soufflé dish. Cover, and freeze, at least 6 hours.

ANNE SAYS
"The mixture should come 1½–2 inches above the rim of the dish so that when the foil collar is removed for serving, the iced soufflé has the raised appearance of a baked one."

4 DECORATE THE SOUFFLE

1 If the soufflé has been frozen more than 1 day, take it from the freezer and let it soften in the refrigerator, about 1 hour. Then carefully remove the foil collar from the dish.

2 Cut the peach in half and discard the pit. Cut each half into thin slices and brush the slices with the lemon juice. Arrange them decoratively on top of the soufflé.

¶◎¶ TO SERVE
Sift the confectioners' sugar around the edge of the soufflé. Place the soufflé dish on a serving plate lined with a napkin, and serve immediately.

Napkin holds soufflé dish steady on plate

V A R I A T I O N

ICED PEACH PARFAIT WITH BLUEBERRIES

Peach soufflé is transformed into a parfait by being swirled with a blueberry compote, then scooped into balls and served with poached peach slices.

1 For the blueberry mixture, put 1 pint blueberries in a saucepan and add 1 tbsp sugar. Heat the blueberries and sugar just until the blueberries pop and the juices run. Taste, adding more sugar as needed. Remove the pan from the heat and let cool.
2 Meanwhile, make the peach soufflé mixture as directed in the main recipe. Pour it into a large bowl.
3 Swirl the cooled blueberry mixture gently into the soufflé mixture. Freeze, covered, at least 6 hours.
4 Using an ice-cream scoop, shape balls of the parfait and divide them among chilled serving plates. Serve at once, with poached peach slices.

STRAWBERRY ICE CREAM IN A FLOWER ICE BOWL

🍴 SERVES 6　🥄 WORK TIME 30–40 MINUTES　❄ FREEZING TIME 8 HOURS*

EQUIPMENT

ice-cream maker

ice-cream scoop

food processor †

candy thermometer

whisk ‡

bowls, including a 9½-inch and a 6-inch bowl

plastic bag

colander

small saucepan

strainer

rolling pin

funnel

dish towels

rubber spatula

† blender can also be used

‡ electric mixer can also be used

Fresh strawberry ice cream looks spectacular in this frosty, flower-studded container. Choose edible flowers with bright colors and bold shapes that will be discernible through the ice. Be sure to allow enough time for the water to freeze solid, and, when serving, set the bowl on a cloth to absorb any drips.

GETTING AHEAD

The ice cream and ice bowl can be frozen up to 1 month. If the ice cream has been frozen longer than 6 hours, let it soften 1 hour in the refrigerator before serving.

* freezing time varies depending on the ice-cream maker you use

SHOPPING LIST

2	handfuls of fresh edible flowers and leaves
36–48	ice cubes
	For the strawberry ice cream
⅓ cup	sugar, more if needed
¼ cup	water
2	egg yolks
1¼ cups	light cream
1 quart	strawberries
2 tbsp	kirsch

INGREDIENTS

edible flowers and leaves

strawberries

sugar

egg yolks

light cream

kirsch †

† lemon juice can also be used

ORDER OF WORK

1 MAKE THE STRAWBERRY ICE CREAM

2 MAKE THE FLOWER ICE BOWL

3 UNMOLD AND FILL THE ICE BOWL

1 MAKE THE STRAWBERRY ICE CREAM

1 Heat the sugar and water in the small saucepan until the sugar has dissolved, stirring occasionally. Boil, without stirring, until the syrup reaches the soft ball stage, 239°F on the candy thermometer.

ANNE SAYS

"To test the syrup without a thermometer, take the pan from the heat and dip a teaspoon in the hot syrup. Let the syrup cool a few seconds, then take a little between your finger and thumb; it should form a soft ball."

2 While the syrup is boiling, beat the egg yolks in a bowl until they are just mixed.

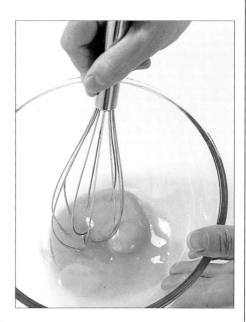

3 Gradually pour the hot sugar syrup onto the egg yolks, beating constantly with the hand whisk or an electric mixer.

! TAKE CARE !

Pour the syrup into the center of the egg yolks so it does not stick to the bowl.

Egg yolk mixture must be cool before cream is added

Pour in cream slowly so it is well incorporated

4 Continue beating until the egg yolk mixture is cool, very thick, and pale, about 5 minutes.

5 Gradually beat the light cream into the thick egg yolk and syrup mixture until it is thoroughly blended.

Ripe strawberries make superb ice cream

Press purée hard to extract all strawberry pulp

6 Hull the strawberries, washing them only if they are dirty. Purée the berries with the kirsch in the food processor. There should be about 2 cups of purée.

7 Strain the strawberry and kirsch purée into the egg yolk and cream mixture, pressing the purée through the strainer with the rubber spatula.

Purée blends with cream to make it rich pink

8 Stir the two mixtures together until they are well blended. Taste, and add more sugar if needed.

9 Pour the blended mixture into the ice-cream maker and freeze it until it is firm, following the manufacturer's directions. Meanwhile, chill a large bowl in the freezer.

10 When the ice cream is firm, transfer it to the chilled bowl. Cover it and freeze at least 6 hours to allow the flavor to mellow. Meanwhile, make the flower ice bowl.

2 MAKE THE FLOWER ICE BOWL

1 Put the flowers and leaves in the colander and rinse very gently but thoroughly to remove any earth and small insects. Spread the flowers and leaves on a dish towel and let dry. Chill the large and small bowls in the freezer.

ANNE SAYS
"Use nesting bowls that are the same shape."

Handle flowers carefully so they are not bruised

2 Put about 24 ice cubes in the plastic bag and wrap the bag in a dish towel. Holding the end of the bag and the towel in one hand, strike the bag with the rolling pin to crush the ice.

3 Put 6–8 ice cubes in the large bowl. Set the smaller bowl on top of the ice cubes, and put a weight in it to keep it in place. Pour enough ice-cold water into the large bowl to fill the gap at the bottom.

Set flower heads downward at bottom of bowl

4 Add a little of the crushed ice to the space between the bowls. Arrange some of the flowers and leaves in the ice and water with their heads or patterned sides facing outward.

Heavy can makes ideal weight

5 Continue adding flowers and leaves with more crushed ice to fill the gap between the bowls. Keep the flowers in place with crushed ice as you arrange them.

At top of bowl, position flower heads pointing upward

6 Pour ice-cold water through the funnel into the gap between the bowls to fill up to the rim of the large bowl. Freeze until completely solid, 3–4 hours.

! TAKE CARE !
The flowers and leaves should be completely submerged. Keep them in place with more crushed ice if necessary.

3 UNMOLD AND FILL THE ICE BOWL

2 Remove the flower ice bowl from the large bowl: wrap a dish towel dipped in very hot water around the bowl to loosen it slightly. Transfer the ice bowl to a serving plate lined with a napkin. Return the flower ice bowl to the freezer until just before serving.

Heat from towel will loosen ice bowl

Do not let ice bowl melt too much

1 If the strawberry ice cream has been frozen longer than 6 hours, transfer it to the refrigerator to soften 1 hour before serving. Remove the flower ice bowl from the freezer. Fill the smaller bowl with hot water, let stand about 30 seconds, then lift off the smaller bowl, with the water.

ANNE SAYS
"The napkin set under the bowl will steady it and absorb drips as it melts."

3 Using the ice-cream scoop, shape the ice cream into neat balls and pile them in the flower ice bowl.

¶◎¶ TO SERVE

Spoon the ice-cream balls into dessert bowls at the table.

V A R I A T I O N
STRAWBERRY-ROSE PETAL BOWL

This version of the flower bowl features scarlet rose petals and green leaves. The ice cream is shaped into small balls and piled high with fresh strawberries.

1 Make the strawberry ice cream as directed in the main recipe. Hull 1 pint additional strawberries.

2 Make ice bowl as directed, using brightly colored rose petals and leaves.

3 Let the ice cream soften in the refrigerator up to 1 hour if necessary, then scoop it into small balls using a melon baller. Arrange the balls on 1 or more baking sheets lined with aluminum foil, then return them to the freezer until ready to serve.
4 Unmold the flower ice bowl as directed. Fill it with the strawberries and small scoops of ice cream.

Bright flowers are natural decoration

Strawberry ice cream will stay chilled in flower ice bowl

DESSERTS KNOW-HOW

No matter what the recipe, fresh, good-quality ingredients are the key to success. This is especially true for desserts, which often use relatively few ingredients. Therefore, the quality of the cream, the fruit, and the chocolate is showcased.

SELECTING INGREDIENTS

To make these recipes accessible to everyone, standard ingredients are used, and an alternative is always suggested for anything that may be hard to find. Eggs should be "large" size, 2 ounces each. Make sure they are clean and free of cracks. I prefer to use whole milk for the ideal smooth texture and full flavor in pastry creams and custards. Cream, whether it is whipped for a mousse or decoration or used to make a sauce or custard, should always be heavy (sometimes called whipping) cream, with a butterfat content of about 40 percent. Unsalted butter is mandatory for delicate cakes and pastries, contributing a sweet, creamy flavor rather than a salty one to the dessert. Fruit should be ripe, juicy, and unblemished when used raw, or slightly firmer for poaching and baking.

All-purpose flour is used for the cakes, pastries, and other recipes in this book. "Sugar" means granulated sugar, unless otherwise stated, and appears in a wide variety of cakes, custards, creams, and meringues. You'll also need confectioners' sugar to make delicate batters and lacy, ethereal decorations. Salt, too, plays a minor role in desserts, and a judicious pinch in cake batters and pastry doughs brings the other flavors into prominence. Do not be tempted to improvise and change the proportions of the basic ingredients in these desserts. Their balance has been carefully tested for optimum results.

SELECTING RECIPES

There's a dessert for every occasion, with a wide choice to suit your budget and to complement the other courses on the menu, whether it is for a simple supper or a grand reception for large numbers. It is important to try and maintain the right balance of advance preparation and last-minute work.

A substantial main course at dinner would be best followed by a light Iced Peach Soufflé or Exotic Fruit in Tulip Cookie Cups. Richer, more elaborate desserts – Chestnut Napoleons or Chocolate Decadence with Raspberry Coulis – should be served at the end of a simpler meal, so guests still have eager appetites to appreciate them fully. As for large numbers, Tiramisù, Mosaic Fruit Terrine, Ginger Cheesecake, or Sour Cream and Fruit Cheesecake are all easy to make in quantity.

Do-ahead desserts give peace of mind to the busy cook, leaving time to enjoy the meal and the company of the guests. Tiramisù, Rum-Soaked Ring Cake, and Baklava all benefit from being made several hours in advance, and so, of course, do the iced desserts. At the other end of the scale, your guests may participate in making their own last-minute dessert, gathered around the fondue pot to dip juicy fruit into warm melted chocolate for Chocolate Nut Fondue.

MICROWAVE

Dessert-makers can happily take advantage of the speed and convenience of microwave cooking for a wide range of techniques. Simple time-savers include melting butter and melting chocolate; the latter should be done at medium power to avoid scorching. Nuts and coconut can quickly be baked until golden brown when spread out evenly on a plate and heated at full power. The tedious chore of blanching and skinning nuts such as hazelnuts can be streamlined by heating them in boiling water at full power for a few minutes to loosen the skins.

GETTING AHEAD

A few desserts, such as Amaretti and Chocolate Bombe and Trio of Sorbets, must, by their nature, be made ahead. Others, such as Mosaic Fruit Terrine, are prepared in advance, then unmolded and sliced at the last minute. Many complicated dessert recipes can be simplified by completing certain components ahead of time. You can bake basic cakes up to two weeks in advance, let them cool, then wrap and freeze them for use in recipes such as Tiramisù, Baked Alaska, and Coconut and Pineapple Mousse Cake. Crêpes freeze well when stacked and wrapped (each crêpe should be separated by a sheet of wax paper), making Crêpes Suzette feasible on a tight schedule. Another good way to get ahead is to make a batch of puff pastry dough and freeze it to use for Chestnut Napoleons or Apple and Almond Galettes. I think of puff pastry in the freezer as money in the bank. Simply thaw the pastry, still wrapped, in the refrigerator overnight, then roll, shape, and bake as directed.

PRESENTING DESSERTS

Dessert is the grand finale, the moment to leave a lasting impression of a delicious meal. At dinner, don't hesitate to bring out your finest platters to display your confections at their best. For maximum impact, I like to make spectacular desserts, such as Hazelnut Meringue Gâteau or Grand Marnier Soufflé, and bring them whole to the table to serve up in front of guests. Other recipes are designed for presentation on individual plates, such as Phyllo Nut Rolls, Rum Babas, or Chocolate Decadence with Raspberry Coulis.

The shape of many desserts is a decoration in itself – the tower of a chilled soufflé, the mosaic in a fruit terrine – and you have the option of adding colorful clusters of fruit, sprigs of mint, rosettes of cream, or a sprinkling of grated dark or white chocolate. You'll find all sorts of ideas if you look through this book. When you're in a hurry, even a simple dusting of confectioners' sugar adds a finishing touch to the surface of cakes and pies. Be aware, however, that decorations often do not last well – sugar melts and mint sprigs wilt in a warm room. So, for safety, turn out and decorate desserts at the last appropriate moment, and then store them in the refrigerator unless otherwise specified.

DESSERTS AND YOUR HEALTH

Many of the basic ingredients in desserts – sugar, butter, cream, chocolate, nuts – are high in calories and cholesterol or saturated fat and are therefore not considered "healthy." But don't be tempted to replace them with low-calorie, low-fat substitutes, since in most recipes the correct ingredients are indispensable to success. By serving moderate portions of these richer desserts, in the context of a healthy general diet, you can enjoy the occasional indulgence without worry.

Luckily, a delicious, mouthwatering dessert need not always be high in fat. For naturally lighter fare, try Mosaic Fruit Terrine, Exotic Fruit in Tulip Cookie Cups (without the cream), or any of the six luscious fruit sorbet flavors in this book, perhaps served in the stunning flower ice bowl featured with Strawberry Ice Cream.

EGGS: HANDLE WITH CARE

There is a very slight risk of salmonella food poisoning from raw or lightly cooked eggs. The bacteria is carried by contaminated hens or may penetrate the egg through a crack in the shell. To minimize the risk, keep eggs refrigerated at 40°F or less. Most recipes in this book require the eggs to be thoroughly cooked, which kills salmonella, so there is no need for concern. However, if you are worried, I suggest you avoid the recipes (and variations) for Tiramisù, Hazelnut Meringue Gâteau, Baked Alaska, Chocolate and Amaretti Bombe, Iced Peach Soufflé, and Strawberry Ice Cream, where the eggs are only lightly cooked. None of the recipes in this book contains raw eggs.

HOW-TO BOXES

In each of the recipes in **Delicious Desserts** *you'll find pictures of all the techniques used. However, some basic preparations appear in a number of recipes, and they are shown in extra detail in these special "how-to" boxes:*

USEFUL TECHNIQUES

The techniques shown on these pages are used in many of the recipes in this book. They are not difficult to master, yet they invariably make a real difference to the appearance, texture, and taste of the finished dish. Follow them with care and they will help you produce delicious desserts with ease.

HOW TO LINE A ROUND CAKE PAN

Lining a cake pan with parchment paper ensures that the cake will not stick. If the batter is rich, the pan should also be floured, so that any excess butter is absorbed.

1 Fold a square of parchment paper into quarters, then into triangular eighths.

2 Hold the point of the triangle over the center of the pan base; cut the paper even with the edge.

3 Melt 2–3 tbsp of butter and brush the pan with an even coating. Unfold the paper and press it onto the bottom of the pan. Butter the paper.

Make sure all excess flour is removed

4 If directed in the recipe, flour the pan: sprinkle in 2–3 tbsp flour, then turn and shake the pan so that the flour evenly coats the bottom and side. Tap the pan to remove all the excess flour.

HOW TO FILL A PASTRY BAG

Chantilly cream and meringue are both suitable mixtures for piping.

1 Drop the tube into the pastry bag and twist, tucking the bag into the tube. This will prevent any mixture from leaking out.

2 Fold the top of the bag over your hand to form a collar and add the cream or meringue, using a rubber spatula or pastry scraper and scraping it against the bag.

3 When the bag is full, twist the top until there is no air left in it. When piping, hold the twisted top of the bag between your thumb and forefinger and squeeze the bag gently to press out the mixture. Do not squeeze the bag with your other hand, but simply use it to help guide the tube as you pipe.

HOW TO SEPARATE EGGS

Eggs are easy to separate if you use the shell. However, if an egg shell is contaminated with salmonella, bacteria can cling to the shell and spread. Alternative methods are filtering the white through your fingers or using an egg separator.

1 **To separate an egg with the shell:** crack the egg at its broadest point by tapping it against a bowl. With 2 thumbs, break it open, letting some white slip over the edge of the shell.

2 Tip the yolk from one half of the shell to the other, detaching the remaining white from the yolk. If yolk slips into the white, remove it with the shell. To remove white threads, pinch them against the side of the shell with your fingers.

To separate an egg with your fingers: crack the egg into a bowl. Hold your cupped fingers over another bowl and let the white fall through them, leaving the yolk.

HOW TO WHISK EGG WHITES UNTIL STIFF

Egg whites should be whisked until they are stiff but not dry. In order for them to whisk properly, the whites, bowl, and whisk must be completely free from any trace of water, grease, or egg yolk. A copper bowl and a large balloon whisk are the classic utensils for whisking egg whites. However, a metal or glass bowl with a balloon whisk or an electric mixer can also be used.

1 Begin whisking whites slowly. When they become foamy and white, increase the whisking speed. If you like, add a pinch of salt or cream of tartar to help achieve maximum volume.

! TAKE CARE !
Do not slow down the whisking once the whites form soft peaks, or they may "turn," becoming grainy.

2 The whites have been whisked enough if they form a stiff peak when the whisk is lifted, gathering in the whisk wires and sticking without falling. The whites should be used at once because they quickly separate on standing.

! TAKE CARE !
Do not overbeat the egg whites; once overbeaten, the correct texture cannot be reconstituted.

HOW TO MAKE CHANTILLY CREAM

Chantilly cream is heavy cream whipped with sugar and vanilla, brandy, rum, or a liqueur. It can be kept refrigerated in a covered bowl, up to 2 hours.

1 Pour the heavy cream into a chilled bowl. Whip with a whisk or electric mixer until the cream forms soft peaks.

2 Add the sugar and flavoring and whip until the cream forms soft peaks again and just holds its shape.

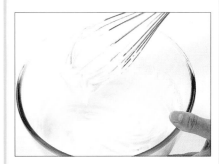

3 Continue whipping until the cream forms stiff peaks and the whisk leaves clear marks.

! TAKE CARE !
If overwhipped, the cream will separate. When this is about to happen, it looks granular.

INDEX

ACKNOWLEDGMENTS

Photographers David Murray
Jules Selmes
Photographers' Assistants Ian Boddy
Stephen Head

Chef Eric Treuille
Cookery Consultant Martha Holmberg
Home Economist Sarah Lowman

US Editor Jeanette Mall

Typesetting Linda Parker
Text film by Disc to Print (UK) Ltd

Production Consultant Lorraine Baird

*Anne Willan wishes to thank Norma
MacMillan and the staff at Carroll & Brown
in London for their vital help in writing this
book and testing the recipes, aided by La
Varenne's editors and trainees.*